PAINTING
Wild Geese

DEDICATION

To the many selfless people who have promoted public awareness of wildfowl carving and painting as a fine art.

ACKNOWLEDGEMENTS

To Ed Flax for the confidence he has shown in me and, to the Art Department of the Martin/F. Weber Company for a job well done.

Featured Wildfowl:

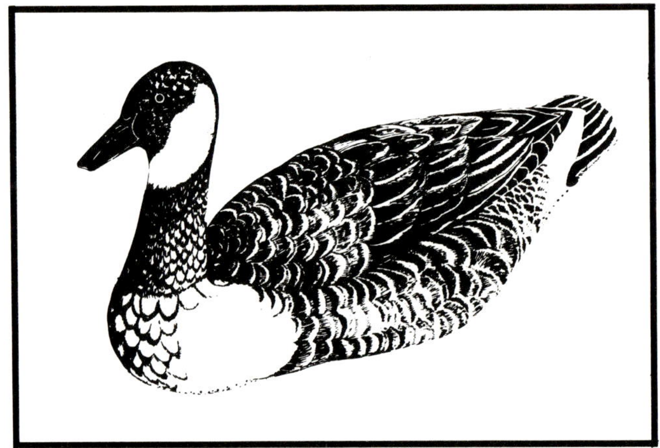

CANADA GOOSE

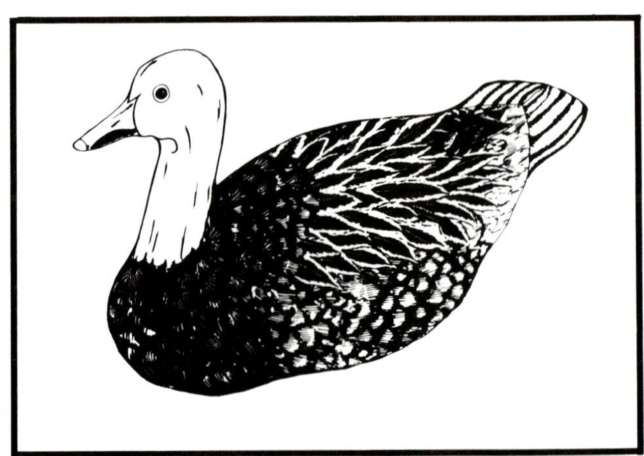

SNOW GOOSE BLUE PHASE

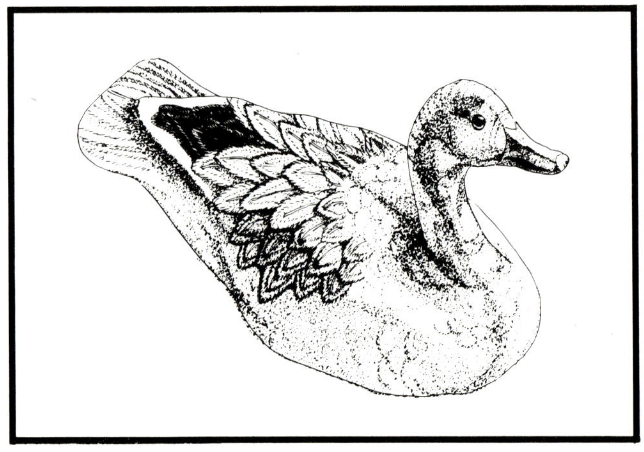

SNOW GOOSE

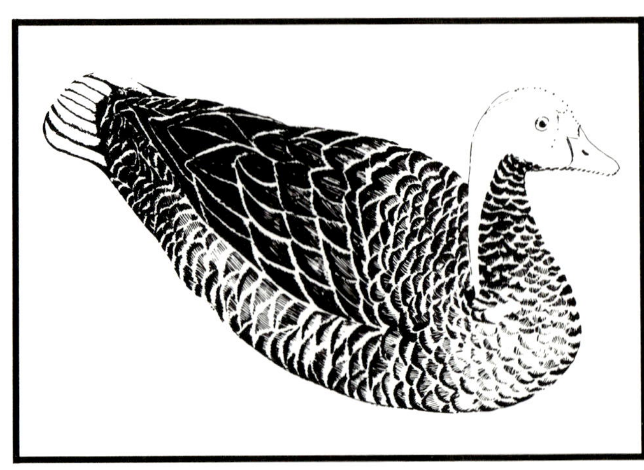

EMPEROR GOOSE

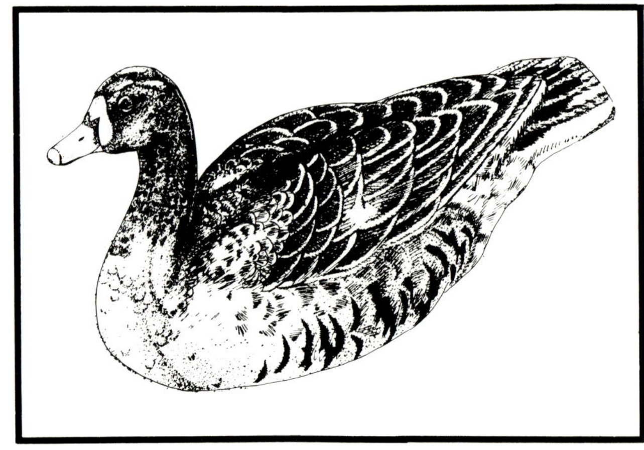

WHITE-FRONTED GOOSE

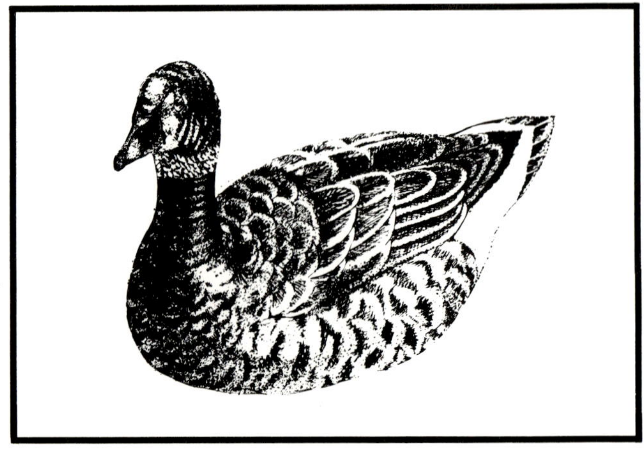

BLACK BRANT

CONTENTS

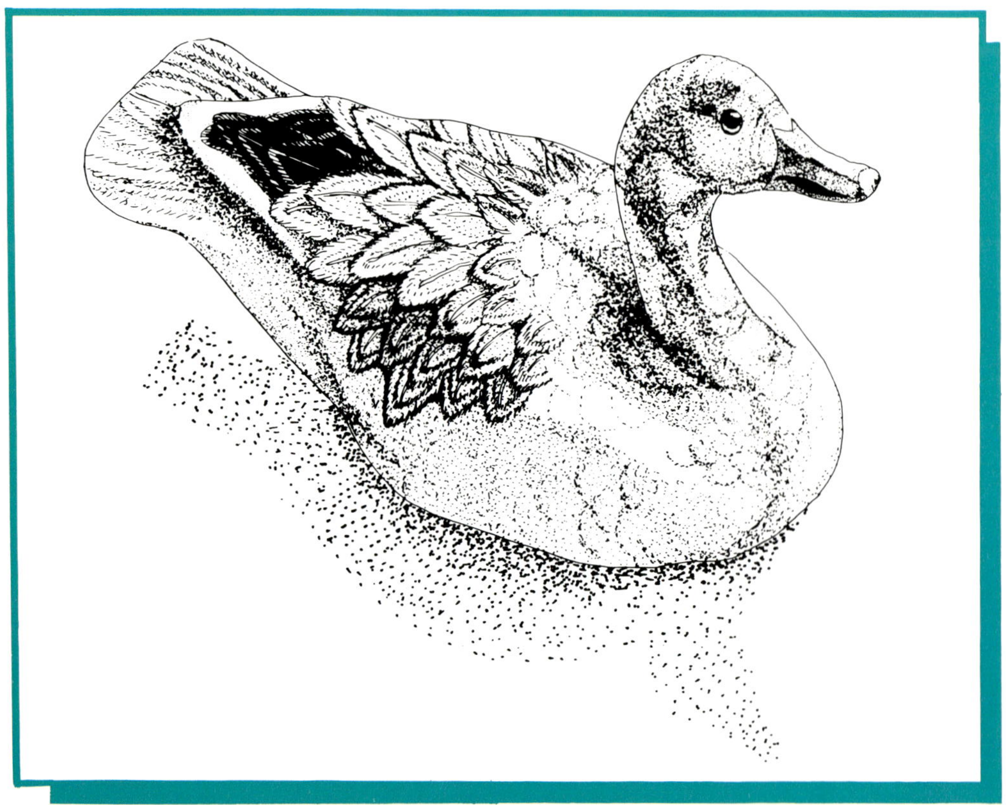

Beebe Hopper is the author of several wildfowl publications which can be purchased at your local art and craft supply store,or write to: Beebe Hopper, 731 Beech Avenue, Chula Vista, CA 92010.

Featherstrokes -- The Basics of Painting Feathers
Featherstrokes for Canvasbacks
Featherstrokes of Mallards
Wildfowl Painting

Beebe Hopper brushes are manufactured by Langnickel, Inc. For further information on these brushes, write to:

Langnickel, Inc.
229 West 28th Street
New York, NY 10001

The decoy blanks shown throughout this publication are courtesy of:

Big Sky Carvers
Bozeman, Montana

Dolington Woodcrafts
Newtown, Pennsylvania

All Permalba Acrylic colors, Permalba matte and gloss medium and support products can be obtained in your local art and craft supply store or by writing to the following address for information on where they can be obtained:

Martin/F. Weber Company
2727 Southampton Road
Philadelphia, PA 19154

A Gathering of Geese

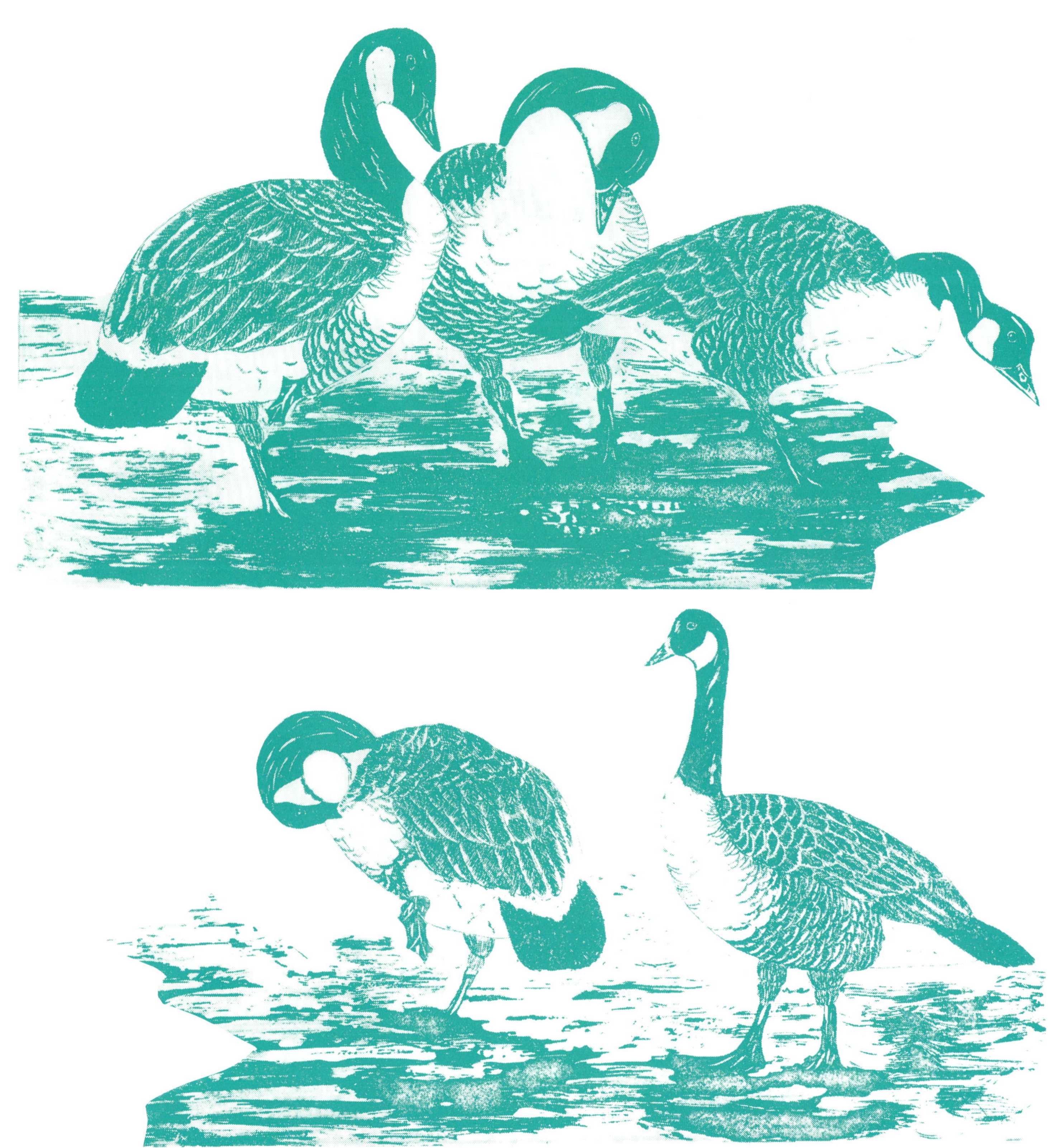

Beebe Hopper

Beebe has always been involved in one form of the art field or another. Upon moving from Mississippi to California in 1950, a whole new world of creative endeavors opened up: ceramics, china painting, crafts of all kinds were introduced to her. Jim, her husband, encouraged her to begin oil painting. Over 20 years ago, she began classes in the adult education system of San Diego County. She fell in love with the arts and has since devoted her time fully to the art field. Watercolor painting, intaglio etching, and acrylic painting of bird carvings are all parts of her creativity today.

Beebe studied at the California College of Arts and Crafts in Oakland, California as well as with such leading artists as Zoltan Szabo, Bennett Bradbury, Bill DeShazo and Bob Landry.

Beebe's work is displayed in the Wildlife Art Museum, Salisbury, Maryland. She is a regularly invited participant for exhibits across the nation including The Waterfowl Festival in Easton, Maryland, The Ward Foundation Carving and Art Show, in Salisbury, Maryland, and the Pacific Southwest Wildfowl Arts, in San Diego, California. Beebe is a consultant to and travels for brush manufacturer, Langnickel, Inc. and for art materials manufacturer and book publisher, Martin/F. Weber Company, demonstrating a simple, easy technique for painting bird carvings in a realistic manner. She conducts seminars in the technique on a nationwide basis.

Beebe's lifelong interest in nature led to the specialization of painting wildfowl and related subjects. Professional organizations with which she is affiliated include the National Wildlife Federation, Audubon Society, Ducks Unlimited, and Pacific Southwest Wildfowl Arts. Beebe is a member of the National Advisory Board of the Ward Foundation, Salisbury, Maryland.

She has authored four publications on how to paint feathers: "Featherstrokes -- The Basics of Painting Feathers", "Featherstrokes for Canvasbacks," "Featherstrokes for Mallards," and "Wildfowl Painting", which was published as both a hard cover and soft cover book. All are excellent foundation material on wildfowl painting.

For thirty-six years, Beebe has been married to Jim Hopper, Commander U.S. Navy (Retired). Upon his retirement from the Navy, he devoted his time to carving birds, most of which Beebe paints. The Hoppers have a married daughter, Holly, and two grandchildren.

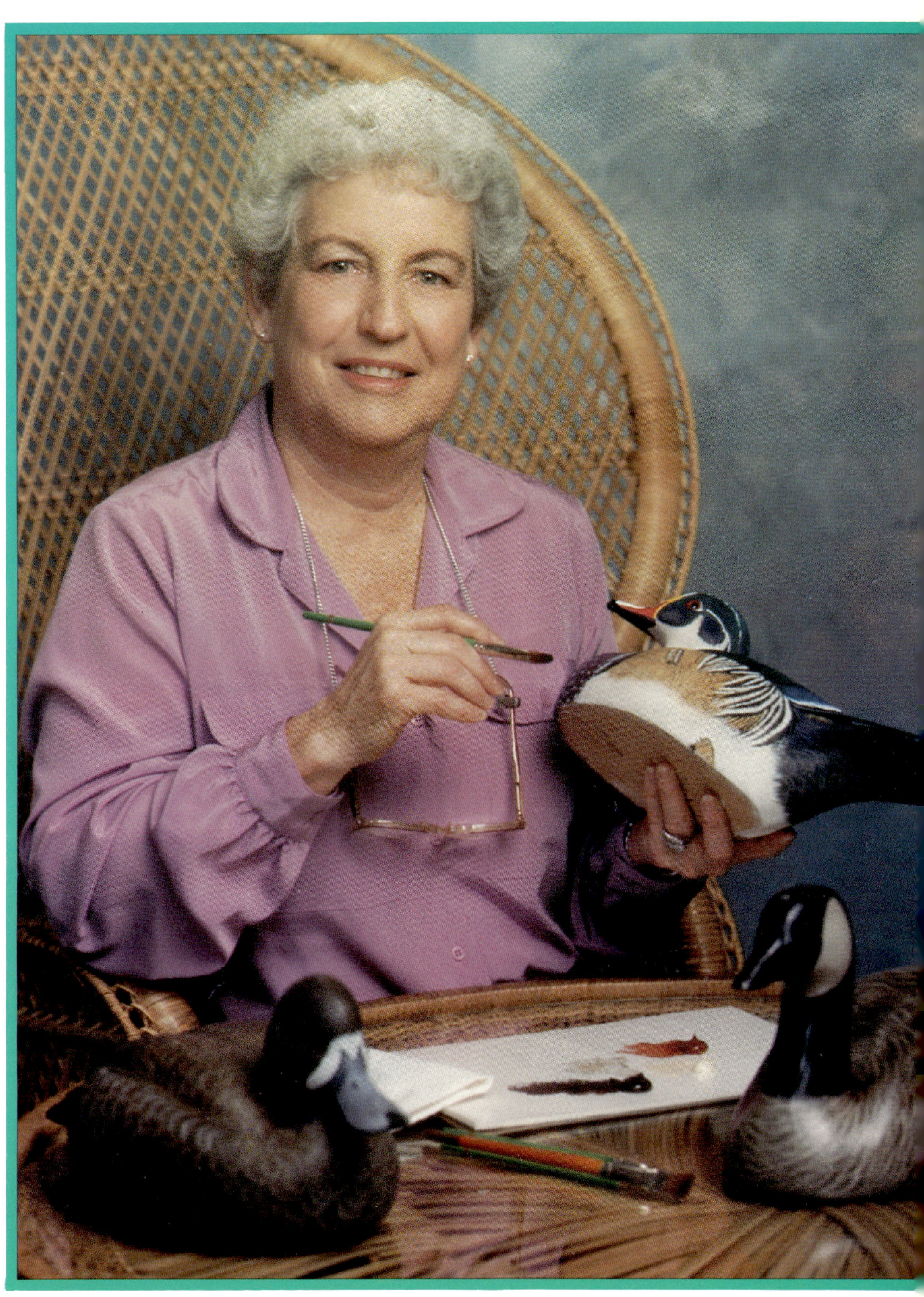

INTRODUCTION

There is an easy way to paint realistic feathers for wildfowl painting! That is what the "featherstroke technique" is all about. The presentation is so simple that anyone who can hold a paint brush can quickly master rendering realistic feathers.

A feather is a feather is a feather, whether it is on a duck, goose, songbird, shorebird, hummingbird, chicken, bird-of-paradise or whatever the species of fowl may be, the feather painting techniques taught in this book are just one approach. They are simple, easy methods which provide the beginner with the background for successful painting from the start. The featherstroke techniques can be used on textured carvings, carvings with the feather pattern burned in, or on smooth surfaces. The techniques can also be used on canvas or other media surfaces, with oils, acrylics, or watercolor. The only difference will occur in the consistency of the paint. Acrylics are the simplest media for the beginner learning these methods. Acrylics hold the bristles of the brush in the desired positions for different shapes and sizes of feather effects. You must work harder at learning and achieving the right consistency for the oil or watercolor medias.

As you experiment and practice mixing and painting with various media, you will develop a "feel" for the paint on the brush and be able to achieve the proper consistency.

Do not be afraid to begin! Remember, it is not yet a great work of art, it is only a piece of wood, canvas or paper! You can repaint it as many times as you choose. Putting this thought into perspective gives you the psychological freedom to begin to create. So why are you waiting?

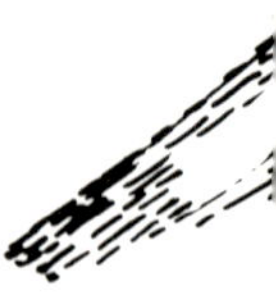

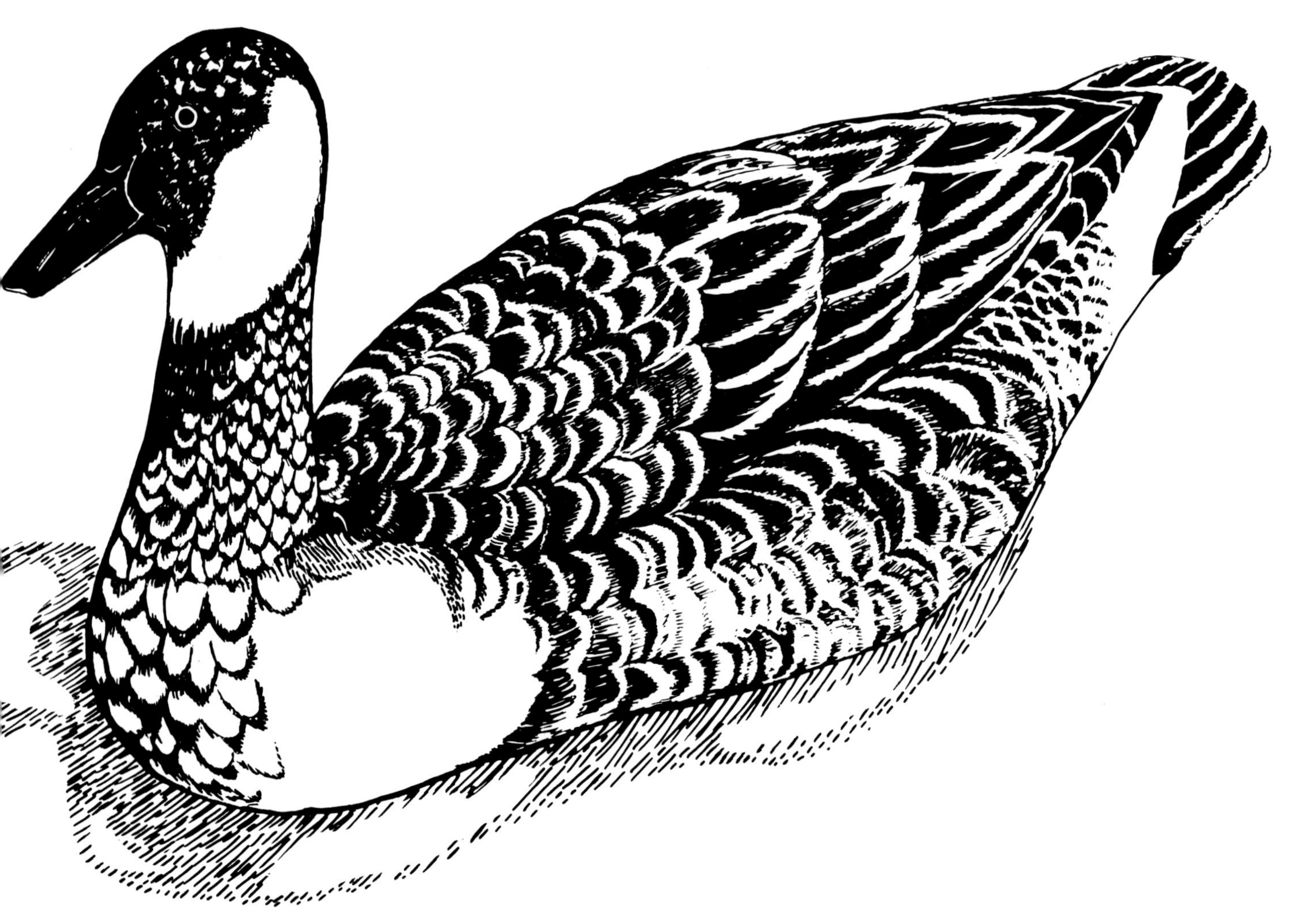

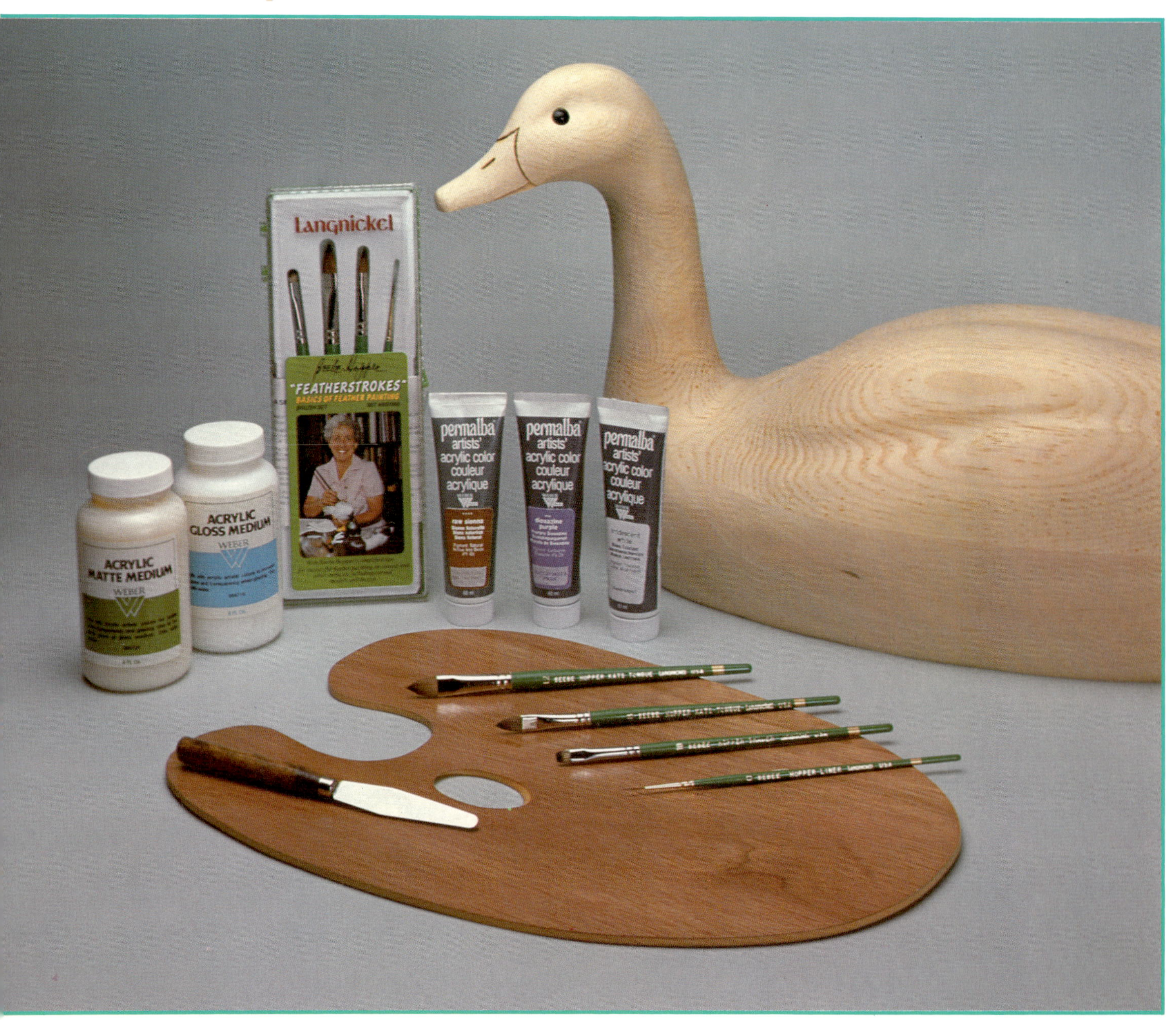

Basic supplies used in painting of wildfowl art.

Supplies used throughout this book are listed below.

MATTE MEDIUM - Used as a finish coat on completed wildfowl carvings.

PALETTE - The wax coated disposable palette is very convenient. A piece of glass with white cardboard or paper underneath provides a firm surface for fanning the Kats Tongue brush.

PAPER TOWELS - Several folded thicknesses of paper towels will be needed for blotting of excess water and paint from your brush.

PAINTING KNIFE - A flat blade knife can be used to mix your colors. Personally, I prefer to mix color with a brush. I feel the color mixed with a brush has more depth and vibrancy.

FINE GRADE SANDPAPER - For smoothing rough areas of carved wildfowl.

WATER CONTAINER - A brush basin, plastic bowl, or glass jar for washing your brushes.

EXACTO KNIFE - To clean the paint off the eyes of the finished carving.

PENCIL - HB or 2B for sketching or drawing on surfaces.

PERMALBA ACRYLIC COLORS

TITANIUM WHITE - A pure white, used alone for highlights or mixed with colors to create tints and hues.

UNBLEACHED TITANIUM - An off-white used with almost any color, especially Raw Umber to create the many shades needed to paint feathers.

RAW UMBER — A dark grayish brown, the most important color in painting most birds. Please note, there is a vast difference in the Raw Umber made by different manufacturers of artists' colors. Permalba Raw Umber has been formulated to properly match the color native to so many birds, whether it is used as a single coat or as a layered wash of color.

IVORY BLACK - A black which is warmer and more transparent than other blacks. A color used to tint other hues and for the application of the darks.

The following colors can be used in the painting of other species of wildfowl.

BURNT UMBER - A rich, dark earth tone brown used throughout wildfowl painting.

BURNT SIENNA - A reddish brown, very warm earth tone applied throughout the painting process.

CADMIUM RED LIGHT - A bright red-orange color.

CADMIUM RED MEDIUM - a rich, intense red mixed with other hues to create some of the bright areas of certain species.

HOOKERS GREEN - A dark, transparent forest green used in certain wildfowl species.

PHTHALO GREEN - A middle value green, toward bluish hue.

PHTHALO BLUE - A middle value blue, vibrant, toward the greenish hue.

ULTRAMARINE BLUE - An intense, bright blue used in the speculum of some wildfowl species.

YELLOW OCHRE - A light, natural earth tone used throughout wildfowl painting.

CADMIUM ORANGE - A bright mid-value orange used in mixtures for color areas such as the bills of wildfowl.

DIOXAZINE PURPLE - A deep, intense purple hue used for the speculum and other areas of some wildfowl species.

CADMIUM YELLOW MEDIUM - A rich, bright middle value yellow for application in color mixtures. A color not typically used alone in wildfowl painting.

METALLIC GOLD - A sparkling, dazzling gold used in feather painting and color mixtures.

IRIDESCENT GREEN - A deep green with sparkling effects used in some head areas of wildfowl species.

IRIDESCENT BLUE - A dazzling blue for application in the speculum areas of some wildfowl species.

IRIDESCENT PURPLE - A deep purple with a rainbowlike glow used in select areas of wildfowl painting.

IRIDESCENT CRIMSON - A vibrant, dazzling red used in mixing of other colors to attain different hues for feathers.

IRIDESCENT WHITE - A pure, white hue with a sparkling glitterlike effect which can be added to a standard color to give iridescence.

PAYNES GRAY - A cool, steel gray applied in the body and bill sections of many of the wildfowl species.

MATERIALS

IMPORTANT! Good tools work for you, inferior tools work against you. So please, have the very best brushes, paints, carving blanks, canvas and paper available. The materials that you use are your tools, and the quality of your work is in direct relationship to the quality of these tools.

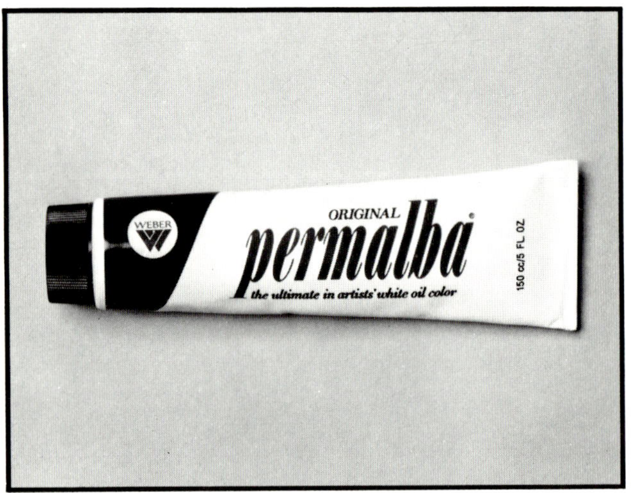

Media

For "painting in the round" (carving and sculpture), I prefer to use acrylics. Fast drying time is the prime advantage of acrylics. It enables you to finish an item without long delays. Drying time is much longer when working with oils. The use of a hair dryer speeds the drying process of acrylics immeasureably. Blending of acrylic colors, however, is a problem for many. A special hint for this is to keep the working areas damp, thus enabling the colors to flow and blend together with ease. Permalba Acrylics, manufactured by Martin/F. Weber Company are paints of superb quality, both in texture and brilliance of hue. The flowing quality from brush to the surface is excellent.
Oil painting on canvas is a very exciting medium, one that enables you to repair mistakes with ease. The vibrance of color and the consistency of Permalba Oils cannot be surpassed.

Brushes

The value of good quality brushes cannot be stressed enough. Many years ago an artist from Palm Springs, California introduced me to Langnickel brushes and it has been a love affair for me ever since. One can pay more for a brush, but one cannot buy a better quality brush than a Langnickel. The Beebe Hopper Feather Painting Brushes are manufactured by Langnickel, Inc. and the Beebe Hopper Kats Tongue has been a mainstay for me when working in oils. When I began painting dimensional carved wildfowl, the brushes adapted so well to realistic feather painting that I felt Mr. Langnickel must have designed them just for that purpose. The Beebe Hopper Shader is ideal for canvas painting, especially for laying in backgrounds. The students and fellow artists to whom I have introduced this brush feel that they do not want to be without it at any time. When this brush is used as a shader for wildfowl feather painting, the results, without a doubt, are unmatchable. The Beebe Hopper Liner works well with all three media: oil, watercolor and acrylic. The bristles are long enough to give the freedom of a rigger brush, but short enough for control of detail work.

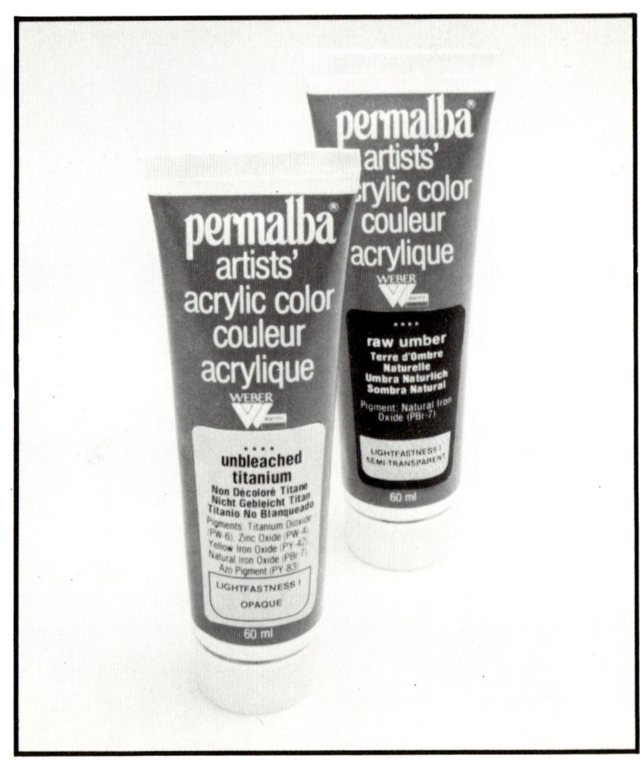

There are three basic elements to each brush: the hair, the metal ferrule and the wooden handle. The hair selected for the head of the brush, animal or synthetic, is the most important element. It must have resiliency, durability and the quality to keep a point or hold a sharp edge.

Brush hair falls into two categories: soft and stiff. Stiff bristles are usually hog or nylon. Soft hairs generally used are kolinsky, weasel, ox, sableline, squirrel, pony and goat. The 'red sable', as it is known to artists, comes from different species of the squirrel, weasel or rodent family which live in cold climates, not from the sable animal.

Various raw brush materials are listed below with a short description of each. Please familiarize yourself with these different types to enable you to distinguish the quality levels of brushes when purchasing them.

KOLINSKY - Known as 'Finest Red Sable', this hair, possessing exceptional spring and fine pointing quality, comes from the kolinsky animal which is native to northern China, southern Russia and Siberia. Only the hairs from the tail are used.

WEASEL - Know as Fine or Good Quality red sable, these hairs come from the tails of the weasel family of animals.

SQUIRREL - A very soft hair taken from tails of different species of squirrel. Painting quality is excellent.

GOAT - A soft hair used in lesser quality or cosmetic brushes.

PONY - From the mane and body of ponies.

HOG - The bristles of the spinal section of wild boars from northern China are used for the top of the line white bristle brushes.

NYLON - A man-made synthetic product used alone or blended with various natural hairs for all styles of brushes. Quality varies a great deal. Until recently, synthetic brushes were not produced at a very high quality level. Today there are some high quality synthetic brushes being produced.

OX - Taken from oxen native to central Europe and North and South America.

SABLELINE - A medium grade hair used for watercolor, lettering, and stroke work. Made from dyed ox hair.

HANDLES - The wooden handles are made from hardwood in either long or short lengths. Wooden handles are usually coated with a sturdy laquerpaint. Plastic handles are generally used with synthetic bristles.

FERRULES - Nickel plated brass or aluminum is used. Most ferrules are seamless to prevent splitting.

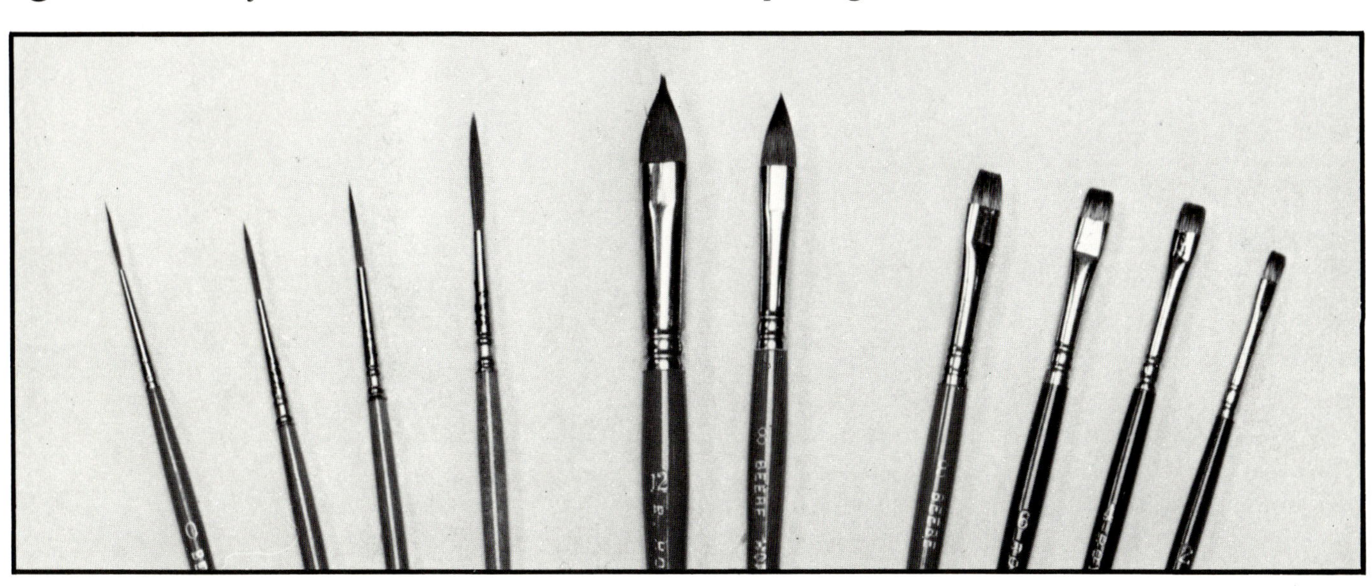

TECHNIQUES AND BASICS

Preparation

To paint a dimensional wildfowl decoy, you must start with a well sanded and primed carved decoy. First, apply a wood sealer to the entire decoy. Let dry. After the carved decoy is sealed, apply a white base primer coat. This can be acrylic, latex paint or a gesso product. After the prime coat has dried, sand smooth with a fine grade sandpaper.

Brush Information

The Featherstroke technique with Beebe Hopper Kats Tongue brush: The Beebe Hopper Kats Tongue brush is simple and ideal to use for painting the individual feathers of the wildfowl. A large size Kats Tongue brush will create very small feathers. On the other hand, a small sized brush will not make feathers larger than when it is fanned to its maximum width. The Beebe Hopper Kats Tongue #12 is used almost exclusively. One exception is for large size carvings such as geese or diving duck hens. A Kats Tongue size #18 is used on these carvings. The Kats Tongue brush will need to be "trained" to hold the proper form. To "train"

this brush, remember to use it in the same direction each time. This is easy to remember if you use it with the writing on the handle facing away from you. Work the brush into the paint and water thoroughly. Fan the brush by press - ing down firmly all the way to the ferrule. Twist carefully back and forth and the brush will form a fan shape. Refer to Photo #1. Slowly draw the brush back and up in the same motion. This is an important stroke motion to learn. Refer to Photo #2. This action will form an arc of the bristles. The brush is now ready to paint featherstrokes. You must remember that a light touch, using thin paint, is necessary when painting feathers. To paint feathers, hold the brush almost upright, and using a flick of the fingers lightly stroke the bristles toward yourself. Refer to Photo #3 and Illustation #1. For creating a sized feather, reduce the arc of the fan by rolling the sides of the brush in - ward. Refer to Photo #4 and Illustration #2. For smaller feathers, reduce the arc again. Refer to

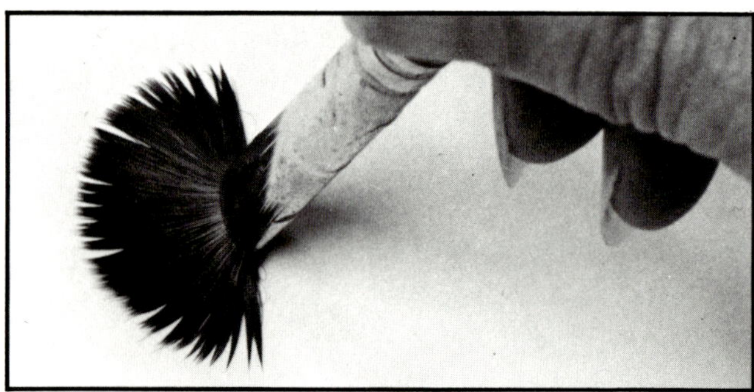

Photo #1
The brush is fanned to its maximum width by twisting the brush back and forth.

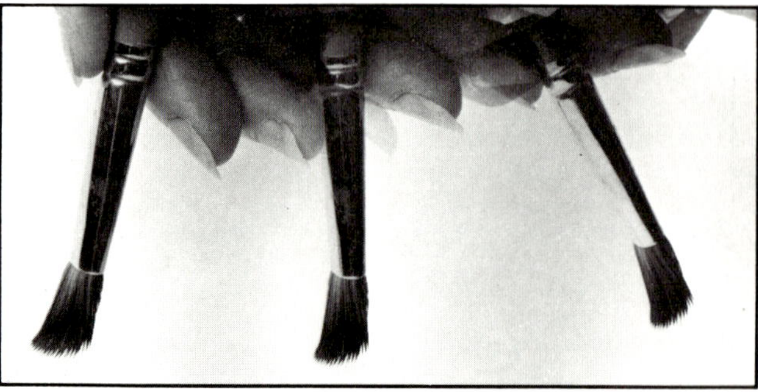

Photo #3
The featherstroke motion is shown above by flicking the bristles of the brush toward yourself.

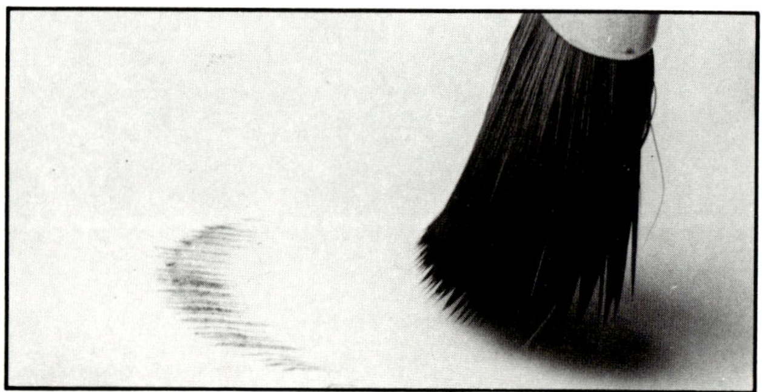

Photo #2
After the brush has been fanned to its maximum potential, release pressure and slowly draw the brush back and up in the same motion.

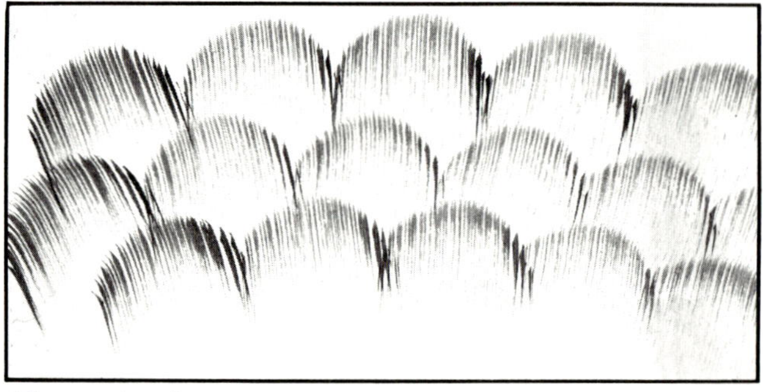

Illustration #1
The featherstrokes shown above were painted using the Beebe Hopper Kats Tongue brush #12 fanned to its maximum potential.

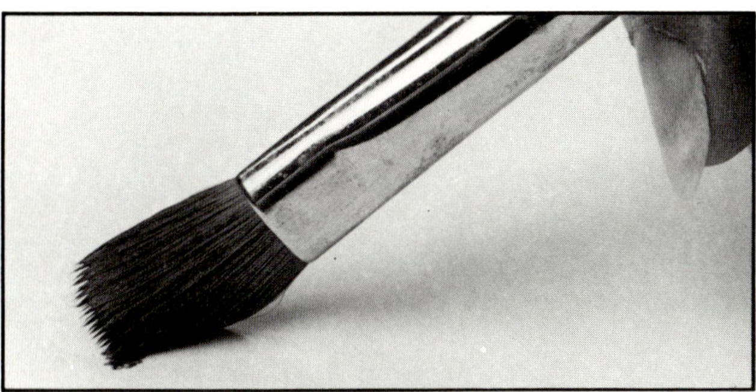

Photo #4
To create medium sized feathers, reduce the arc of the fanned brush by rolling the sides of the brush inward.

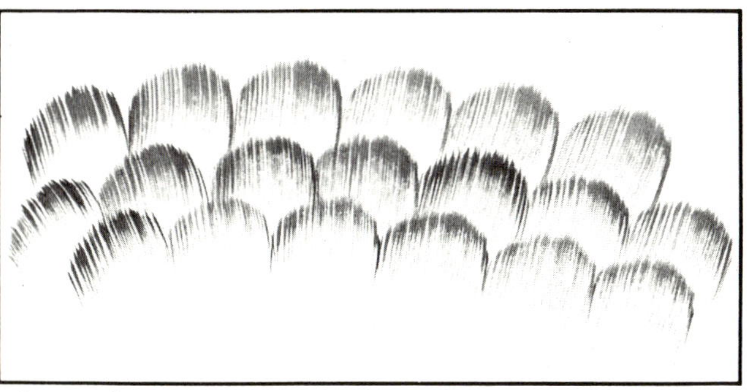

Illustration #2
The featherstrokes shown above were painted using the Beebe Hopper Kats Tongue brush #12 rolled inward to a medium size.

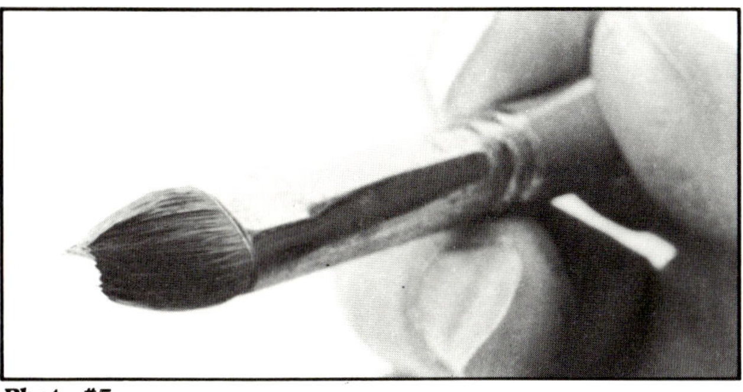

Photo #5
The arc of the brush is reduced again by rolling the sides of the brush.

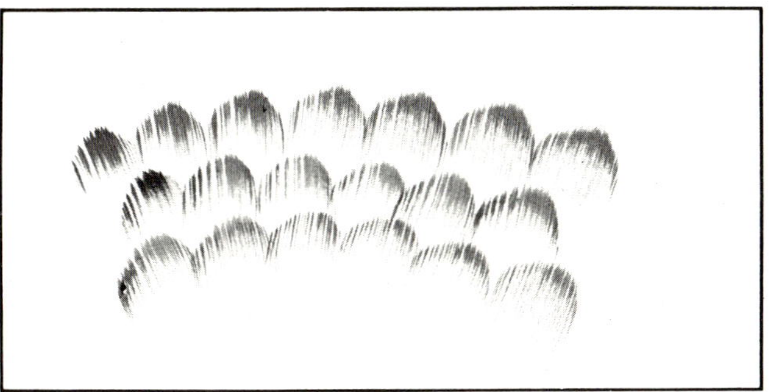

Illustration #3
The featherstrokes shown above were painted using the Beebe Hopper Kats Tongue #12 rolled to a small size.

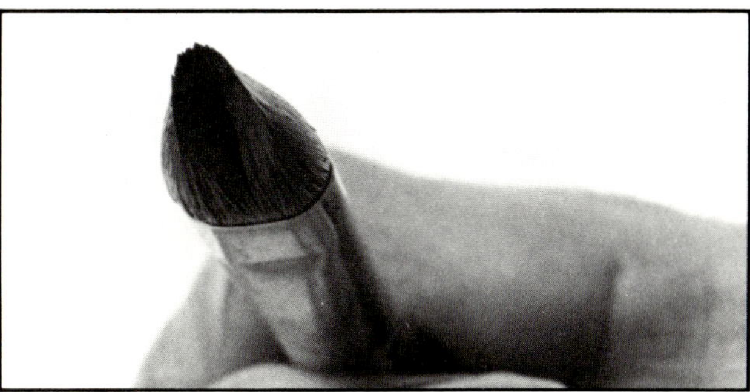

Photo #6
To create the smallest featherstroke with the #12 brush, make a "Tent" or inverted "V" out of the brush tip.

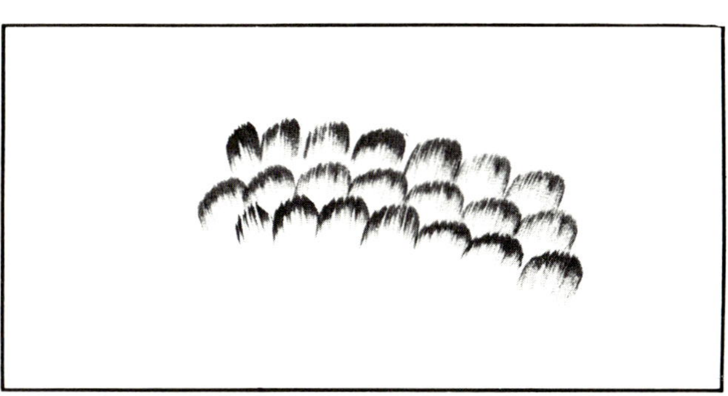

Illustration #4
Featherstrokes painted with the #12 brush with "tent" or inverted "V" shape

Photo #5 and Illustration #3. To paint tiny feathers for the head and neck of the wildfowl decoys, press the sides of the arc together with your fingers to form a "tent" or inverted "V". Refer to Photo #6 and Illustration #4. Hold the brush perpendicular to the surface and with a light touch, paint the tiny feathers. If bristles split or separate, use more paint, but only enough to hold the bristles in the desired position. The angle of the brush when drawing back and up off the palette determines the deepness or shallowness of the arc of the featherstroke. When the handle is at a higher angle, the featherstroke arc is deeper. Refer to Photo #7. When the handle is at a lower angle, the arc of the featherstroke is more shallow. Refer to Photo #8.

TECHNIQUES AND BASICS

LINEWORK

The Beebe Hopper Liner brush is used for fine line detail of carvings and also makes great grass and twiggy trees in landscape painting. To complete the linework technique, the paint should be the consistency of ink. Saturate the brush with thin paint, brace your hand and use only the tip of the brush. Refer to Photo #9 and Illustration #5. It works like a fountain pen. The paint keeps flowing down to the tip. When lifting off the palette, roll the brush and lift to form a sharp point.

SHADING

The Beebe Hopper Shader Brush is ideal for canvas painting, especially for applying foundations in backgrounds. The students to whom I have introduced this brush feel they cannot paint without it. The bristles come to a fine razor edge and are used for shading on the elongated feathers of birds. Refer to Photo #10 and Illustration #6.

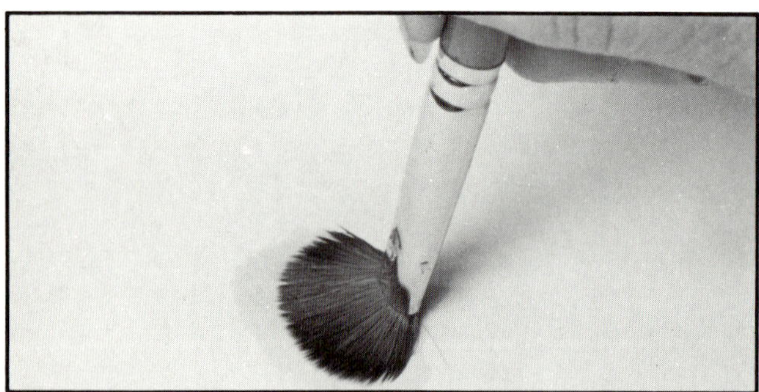

Photo #7
To create a deeper featherstroke arc hold the brush handle at a higher angle.

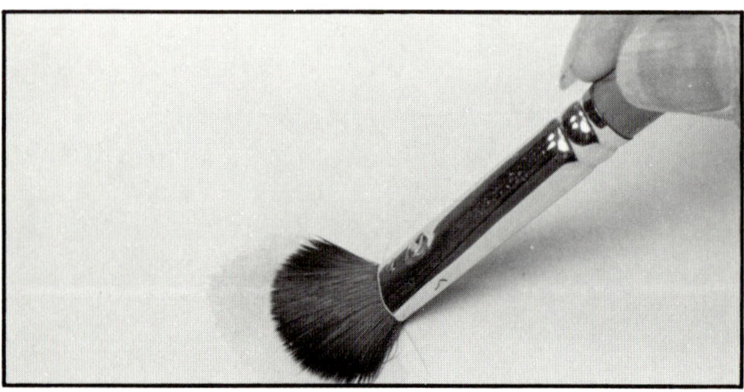

Photo #8
To create a shallower featherstroke arc, hold the brush handle at a lower angle.

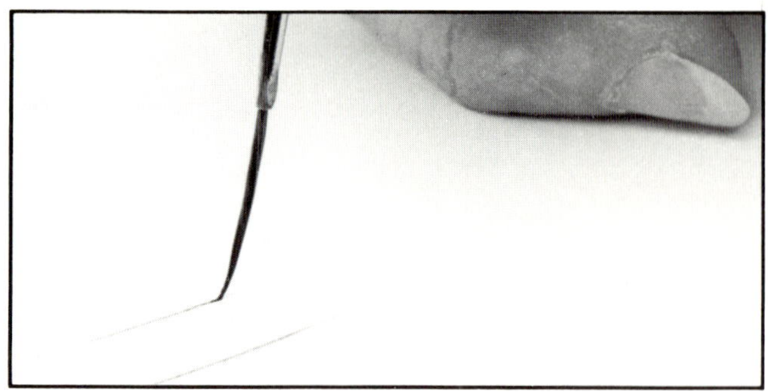

Photo #9
Use only the tip of the Liner brush to paint the linework and detail areas.

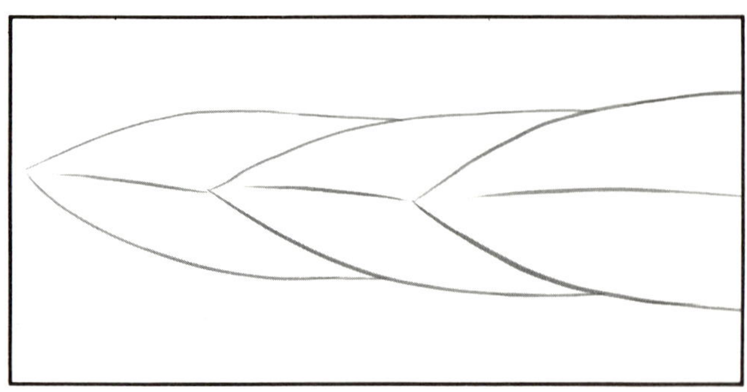

Illustration #5
Linework created to outline the feathers of the wildfowl is accomplished by stroking from the edge of the feather toward the center.

WASHES

A wash simply means a small amount of paint mixed into a larger amount of water. There are thin washes, medium washes and heavy washes. It is difficult to define exact amount. A "rule of thumb" for a thin wash is one drop of paint to thirty drops of water; for a medium wash, the procedure would be more paint into the water; and, for a heavy wash, even more paint mixed into the water. Refer to Illustration #7.

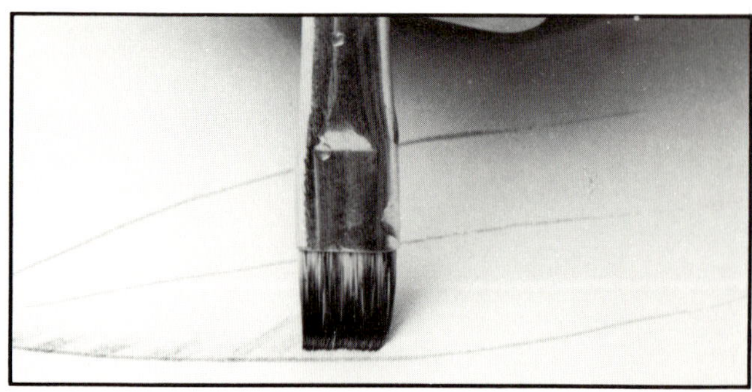

Photo #10
Shading the elongated feathers of the wildfowl is accomplished by stroking from the edge of the feather toward the center.

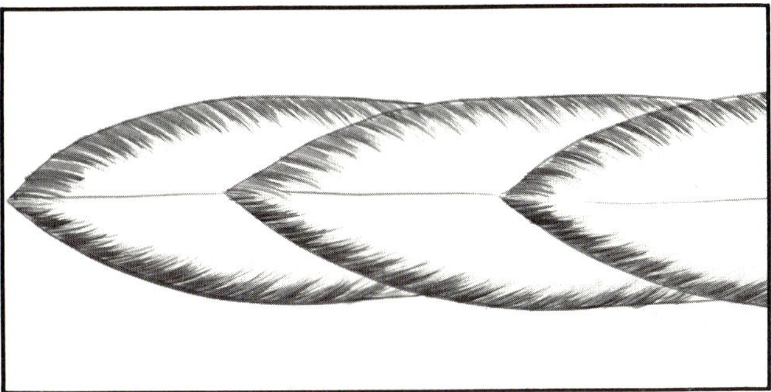

Illustration #6
Elongated feathers shaded at the edge with the Beebe Hopper Shader brush #10.

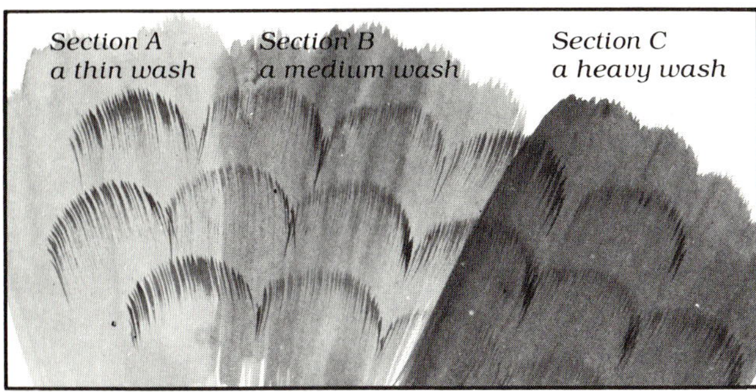

Illustration #7
Applying washes at varying degrees, of opacity can be accomplished by changing the amount of pigment and water.

FINISHING

One way to finish a carving is by applying a generous coat of acrylic matte medium over the completed bird. This gives a satin finish, neither dull nor glossy. The acrylic matte medium looks very milky upon application, but when dry becomes transparent. Apply the acrylic matte medium in a very even application with a soft hair varnish brush or sponge brush.

GLOSSARY OF BIRD DEFINITIONS

BARBS — The part of the feather attached to the quill.

BREAST - Front chest area of bird.

COVERTS - Feathers at the base of the upper tail, also at base of underneath tail area.

CREST - Long feathers at the base of the head and neck.

CROWN - Forehead and top of the bird's head.

DIVING DUCK - Species that dives into the water for food. In order to fly from water, it must take off by running across the water. The legs of a diving duck are further back on the body than a puddle duck.

DRAKE - A male duck.

EYE TROUGH - A recessed area in the front and back of the eye.

HEN - A female duck.

IRIDESCENCE - Shimmering metallic colors on feathers.

JOWL - Jutting part of the jaw.

NAIL - The hardened area at the tip of the bill.

NECK RING - A narrow band of colored feathers around the throat.

PRIMARIES - The ten largest flight feathers of the wing.

PUDDLE DUCK - A species that feeds in shallow water usually by tipping the head into the water while the tail is up in the air. To fly off the water they spring upward. Their legs are toward the center of the body.

SECONDARIES - The ten smaller feathers of the inner wing. (Speculum).

SIDE POCKET - Recessed area between side and back of the duck.

SPECULUM - The brilliant colored smaller feathers of the inner wing.

TERTIALS - Larger feathers of the inner wing.

VERMICULATION - Winding and wavy lines like the track of worms that appear on the feathers of many species of wildfowl.

TIPS

CONTOUR OF FEATHER -
REFER TO ILLUSTATION #8 A & B

1) Always keep your brushes clean!! Wash them thoroughly with soap and water to remove all color, especially near the metal ferrule. Rinse the brush thoroughly and shape it with your fingers to form the natural shape.

2) MOTH PROOF YOUR BRUSHES!! Moths love good, natural hair brushes, especially red sable. When you do not use your brushes often, please store them in a moth proof area.

3) When using acrylics, a few drops of detergent added to the painting water helps to remove pigment when changing from one color to another.

4) Each coat of acrylic must be thoroughly dry before applying the next coat, whether it is a wash or regular coat of paint. If not, the wet coat underneath will come off and you will have an area to repair that takes both time and effort.

5) Permalba Acrylics will not hurt your red sable brushes, *if you keep your brushes clean!* Dried acrylic paint in brushes is very difficult to remove. There are several products on the market which soften hardened acrylic. Check with your local art, craft or tole and decorative painting shop for these products. Rubbing alcohol will soften hardened acrylic. Soak your brushes and with effort you can reclaim them.

6) The side feathers of a goose are round feathers. Those at the back of the goose are slightly squared.

7) REMEMBER! The end of the feather always points toward the tail of the bird, otherwise, the feather will appear to be growing backward on the bird.

8) Painting strokes should follow the contour of the bird. The contour directions of the feathers of wildfowl are illustrated above. Refer to Illustration #8, A and B.

9) Feathers should connect, both front and back and side to side. No open "rows" of feathers should occur.

10) Collect reference material. Begin a library of bird books or any subject in which you are interested. Pictures from magazines, papers, and books are good sources from which to collect.

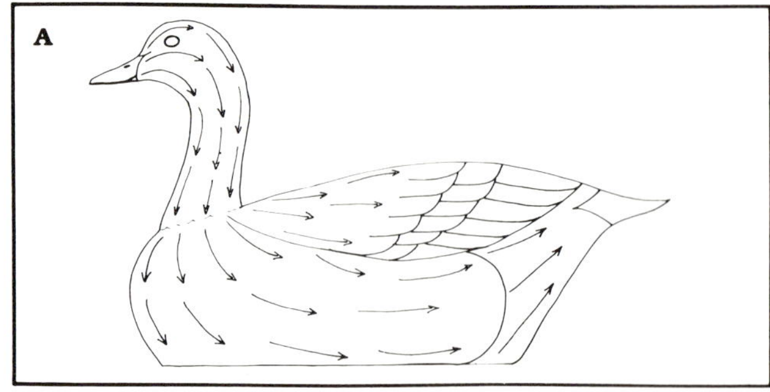

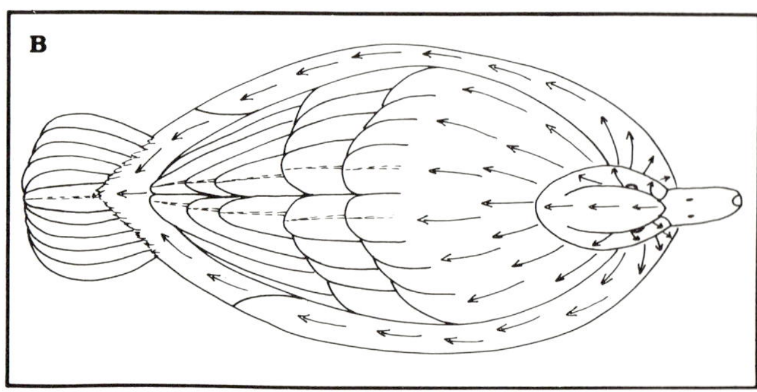

Illustration #8 , A and B
Feather contour directions (Side and Top view) are shown above for featured geese species.

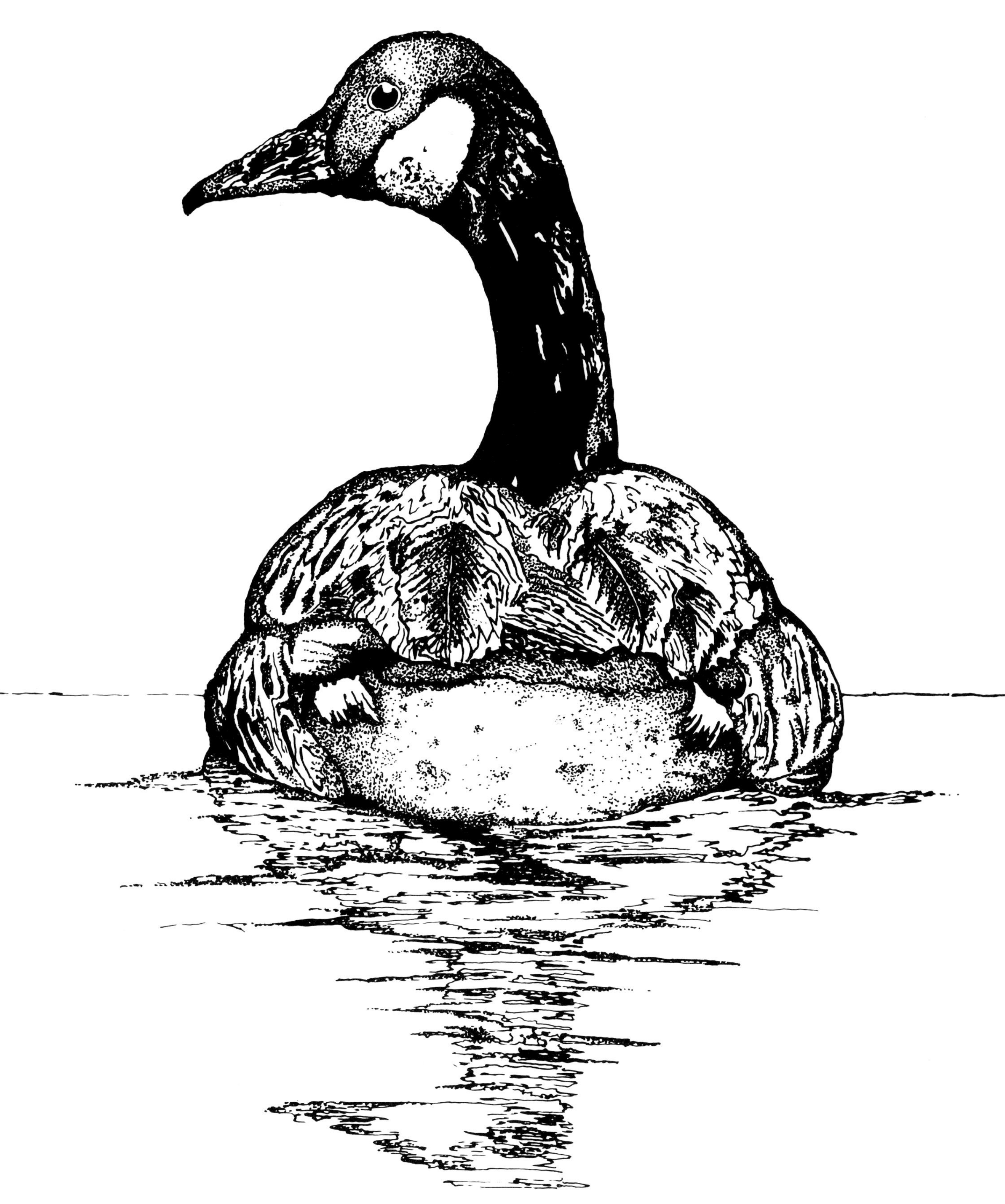

CANADA GOOSE

The Canada Goose is a fascinating bird and rates among the top as the favorite species of wildfowl with bird enthusiasts. Highly intelligent and normally quite long lived, he is monogamous; he mates for life. Should the mate be injured or killed, the survivor frequently will lose its life rather than desert the mate. However, if separation for any reason should occur, they do pick a new mate at a later time.

Canada Geese fly in low, weaving, undulating skeins, one slightly behind and to the side of the bird in front of him. The strongest and wisest are at the head of the "V" formation to break the air passage for the rest of the flock to move forward with less effort. The birds who follow ride the air currents produced by the bird in front. When the lead bird tires, he drops back and the next strongest will take his place.

The Latin name for the species is Branta canadensis. The giant Canada goose is the largest of the species with a wingspread sometimes in excess of six feet. There are several sub-species, all with similar markings. The distinction between the sub-species is the difference in shades of body color and in size. These sub-species include Western Canada, Cackling, Richardson's and Lesser Canada.

There is nothing more exhilarating than to observe a flock of Canada Geese either flying in formation or resting and socializing as only Canada Geese can.

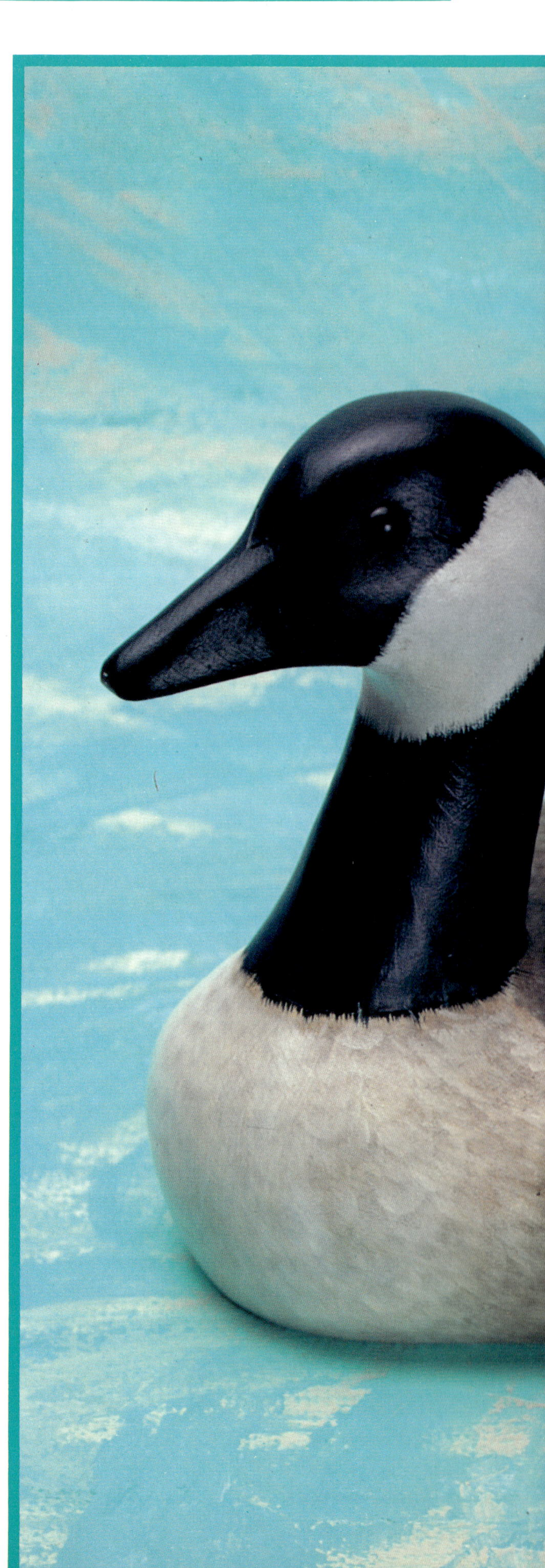

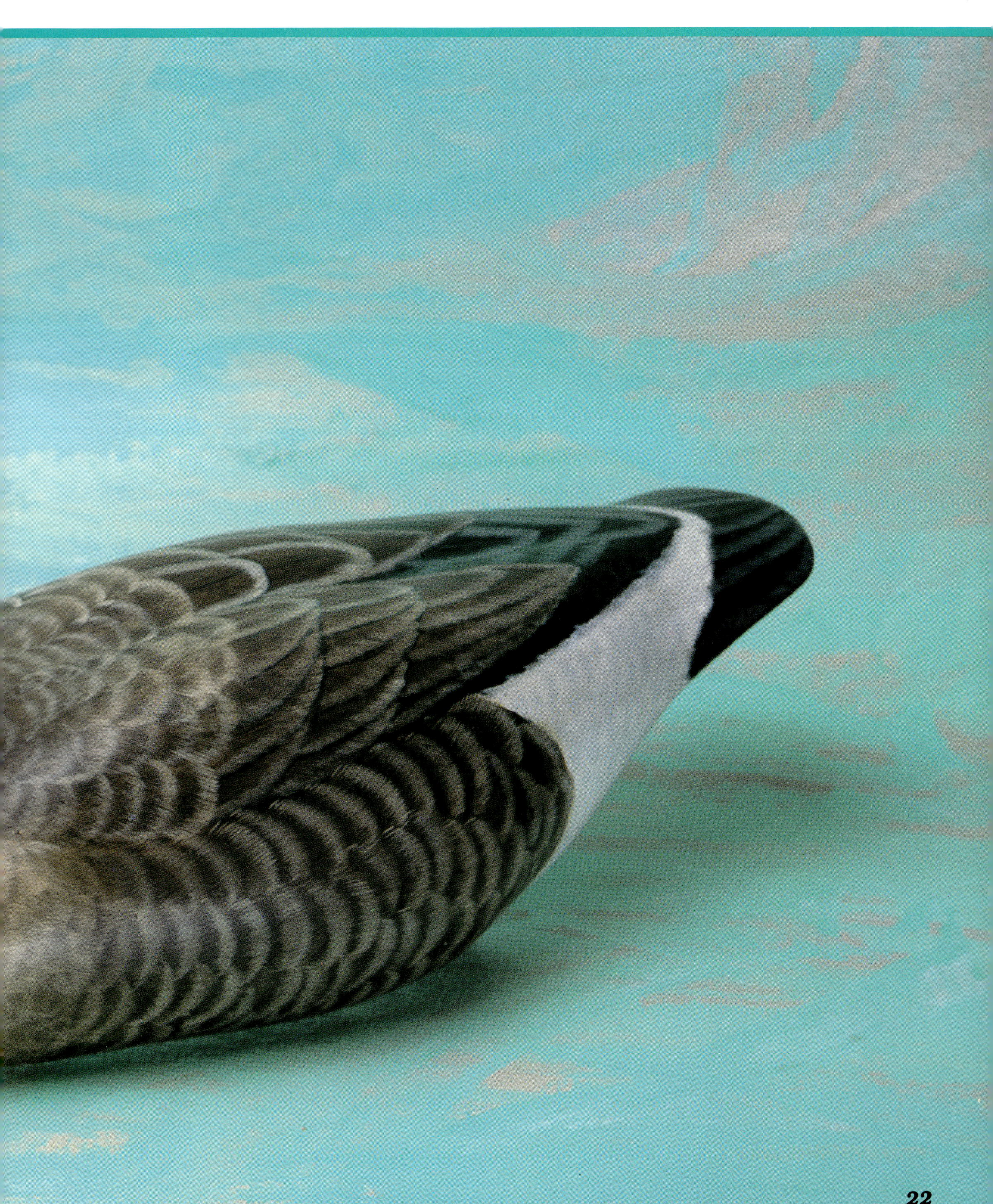

CANADA GOOSE

Permalba Colors

Ivory Black
Titanium White
Raw Umber
Unbleached Titanium

Brushes

Beebe Hopper Liner #0
Langnickel 533T #18
Beebe Hopper Shaders #10 and #14
Beebe Hopper Kats Tongue #12

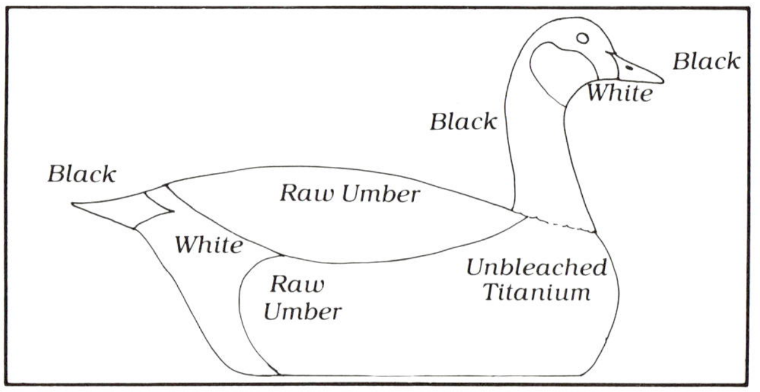

Illustration #9
Color placement diagram (Side view). Follow diagram to outline areas of color.

Before beginning to paint the Canada Goose, sand the blank smooth. Then apply a wood sealer to the entire blank and let dry. After the piece is sealed, apply a prime coat of paint. Let dry and sand lightly to create a smooth surface.

Draw in the abstract areas to be painted using Illustration #9 as a guide.

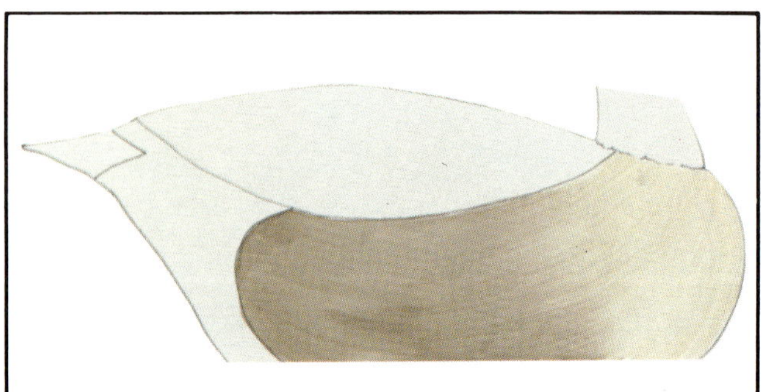

Illustration #10
Carefully blend Raw Umber forward from side flanks of Canada Goose into Unbleached Titanium on chest to achieve a smooth transition of color.

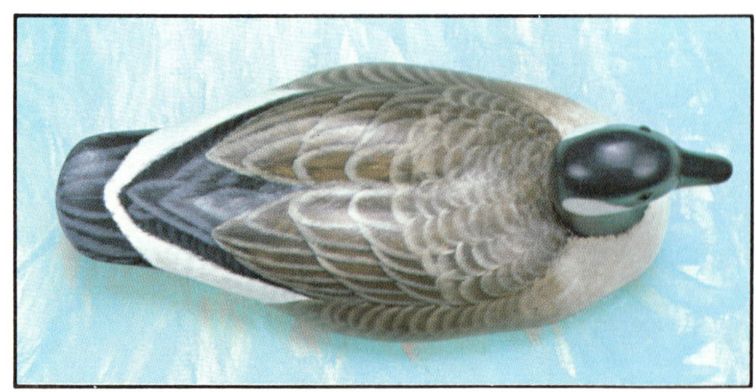

BACK, SIDES AND SHOULDERS

Paint all of back using Raw Umber fairly thin. Paint the side flanks using Raw Umber, then paint the chest using Unbleached Titanium. Carefully blend the two colors in the area depicted by Illustration #9. Refer to Color Illustration #10.

Draw in feather pattern on back, sides and shoulders using Illustrations #11 and #12 as a guide.

The feather arc on the sides and shoulders of geese is much shallower than on other waterfowl; therefore, I use the Kats Tongue #18 with a shallow arc for painting these feathers. Refer to Photo #8. The feather pattern for the back and sides should be completed before each wash is applied.

Using thin Unbleached Titanium, brush on feather pattern with the Langnickel Kats Tongue #18 fanned until desired arc is achieved.

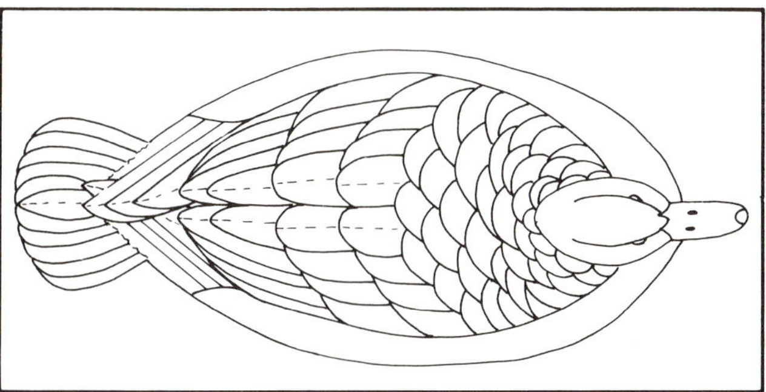

Illustration #11
Feather placement diagram (Top view). Follow diagram for general placement of featherstrokes on primary and tail sections.

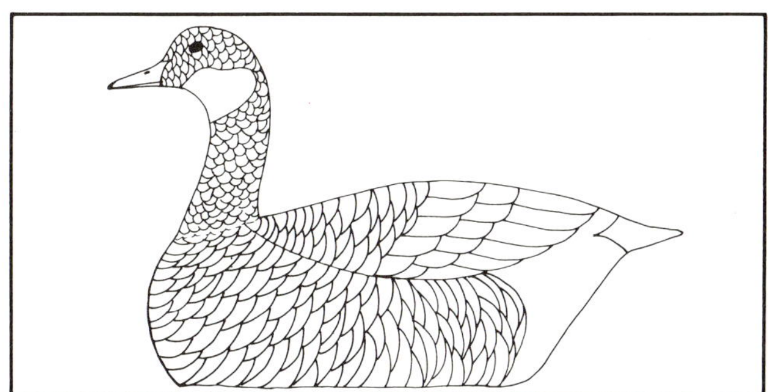

Illustration #12
Feather placement diagram (Side view). Follow diagram for general placement of featherstrokes on head, neck, wing and tail areas.

Illustration #13
Apply layers of feathercoats and washes on lower back areas until desired softness is achieved.

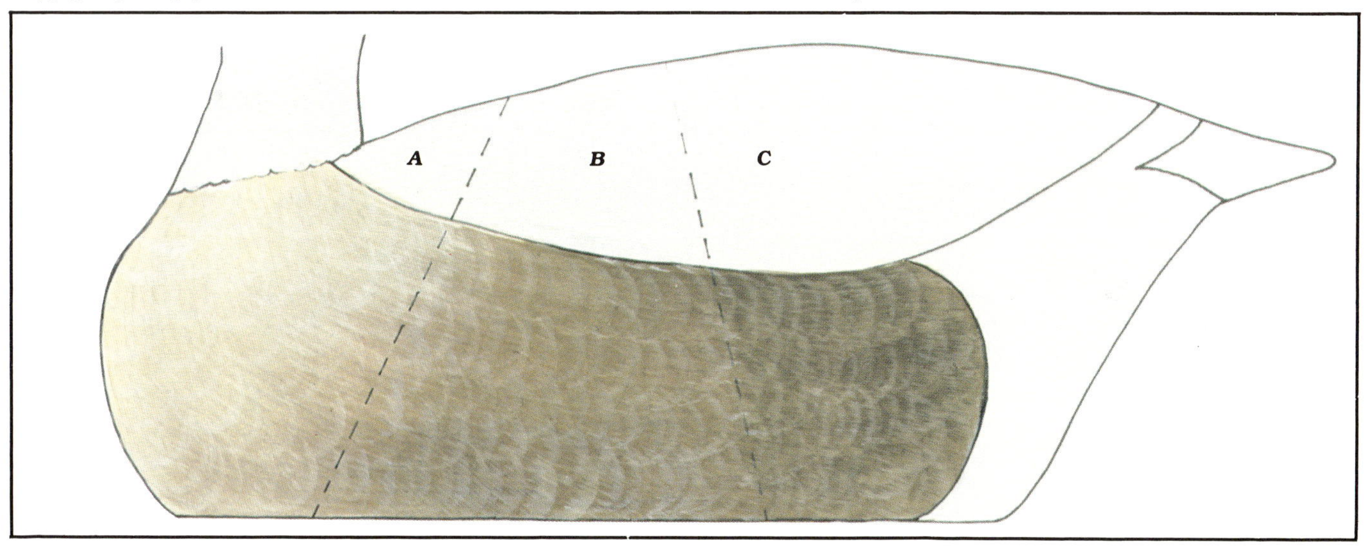

A. *1 feathercoat*   **B.** *2 feathercoats*   **C.** *3 feathercoats*
   1 wash   *2 washes*   *3 washes*

LARGE, LOWER BACK FEATHERS

From the outer edge, stroke inward with Unbleached Titanium using Shader Brush #14. (On large feathers and birds, the larger the shading brush used, the fewer strokes needed.) Apply these strokes with a very light touch. When the feather pattern is dry, apply a wash of Raw Umber to back, flanks and shoulders. A lighter thin wash of Unbleached Titanium is applied to the chest area blended into the Raw Umber wash.

Continue layers of feather patterns and washes until desired softness is achieved. Refer to Illustration #13.

HEAD, NECK AND CHEEK PATCH

Paint cheek patch with white strokes following contour of feathers.

Coat head, neck and bill with several thin coats of Black. This gives more life to the paint than one thick coat. Stroke in a ragged edge between neck and chest to avoid a harsh line between sections. To create a feather pattern on the head and neck, mix a tiny amount of Unbleached Titanium with black to make a dark gray, just slightly lighter than the black. Using the Beebe Hopper Kats Tongue #12, reduced to small size, make feather pattern over head and neck following contour of feathers. Should the feather pattern be too light or harsh, use black as a wash to subdue.

CANADA GOOSE

RUMP

Using Titanium White with a touch of Unbleached Titanium to dispel the chalky appearance, paint the top and bottom of the rump. To create a feather pattern, use white with a tiny amount of Black to make a *light* gray, just slightly darker that the white. Using the Beebe Hopper Kats Tongue #12, make a feather pattern over the area following the contour of feathers. Refer to Illustration #14.

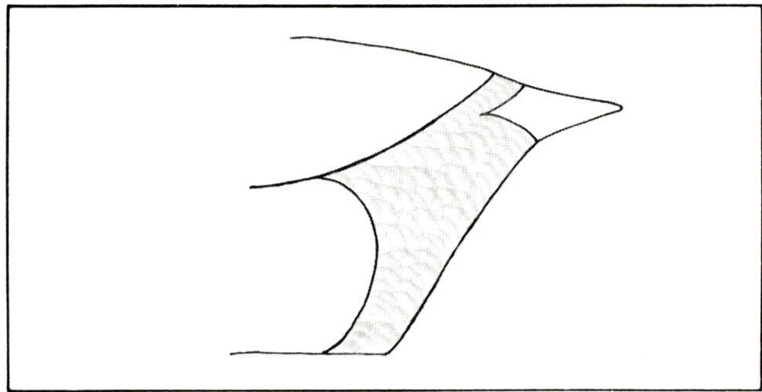

Illustration #14
Refer to the contour of feather placement for rump area of Canada Goose

TAIL

Paint tail Black using several thin coats. Draw in feather outline sections on top and bottom using the Beebe Hopper Liner #0. Refer to Illustrations #15 and #16. Using the Beebe Hopper Shader #10 or #14 and the dark gray mix, stroke inward from outer edge using thin paint and soft strokes. Refer to Illustration #16.

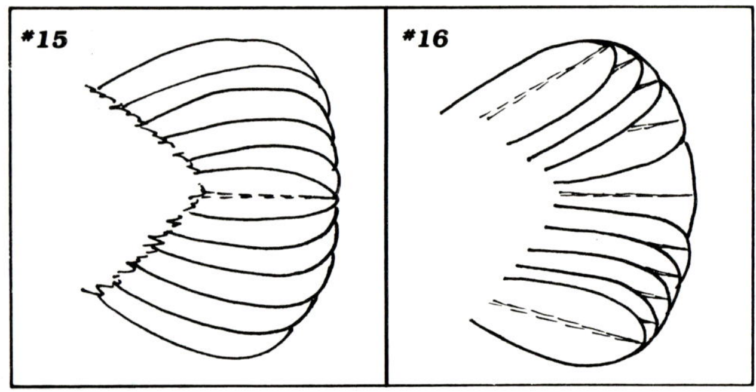

Illustration #15
Feather placement diagram (Top view). Follow diagram for general placement of featherstrokes for tail section.

Illustration #16
Feather placement diagram (Bottom view). Follow diagram for general placement of featherstrokes for primaries.

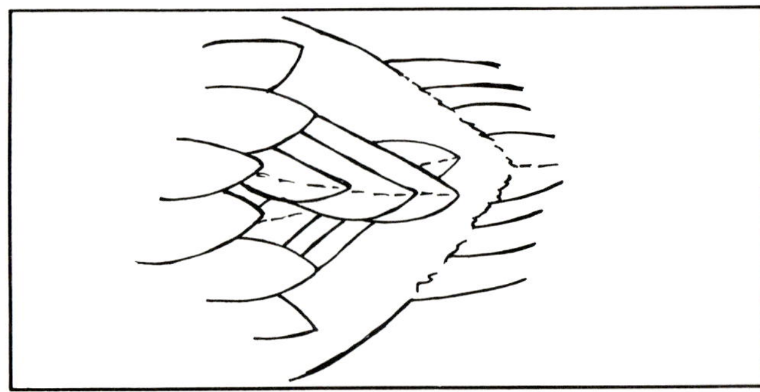

Illustration #17
Feather placement diagram (Top view). Follow diagram for general placement of featherstrokes for primaries.

PRIMARIES

Referring to Illustration #17 as a guide, draw in the primary feather area. Paint area with Raw Umber; then, using the Beebe Hopper Liner #0, draw in feather detail with Black. Shade inward from outer edge with thin Unbleached Titanium using the Beebe Hopper Shader #10. Wash with Raw Umber to soften.

BILL	EYE
Black	Brown

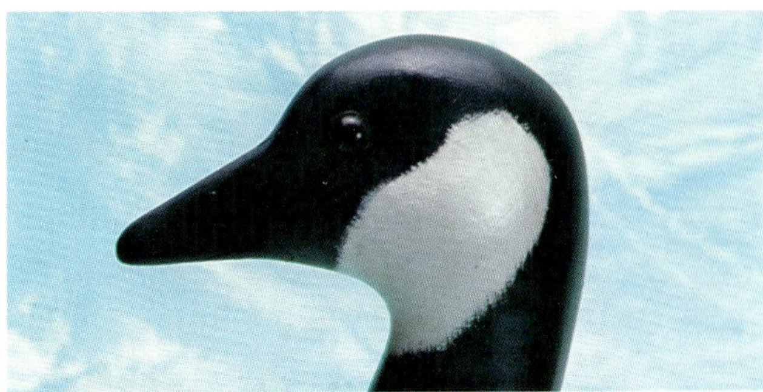

Detail - *Head and Tail Area*
The head area of the Canada Goose is black with subtle featherstrokes and its telltale white cheek patch. Carefully bring some of the tail color into the white of the rump.

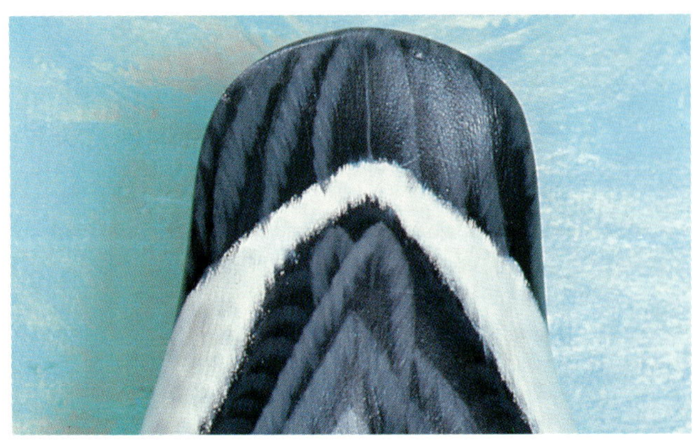

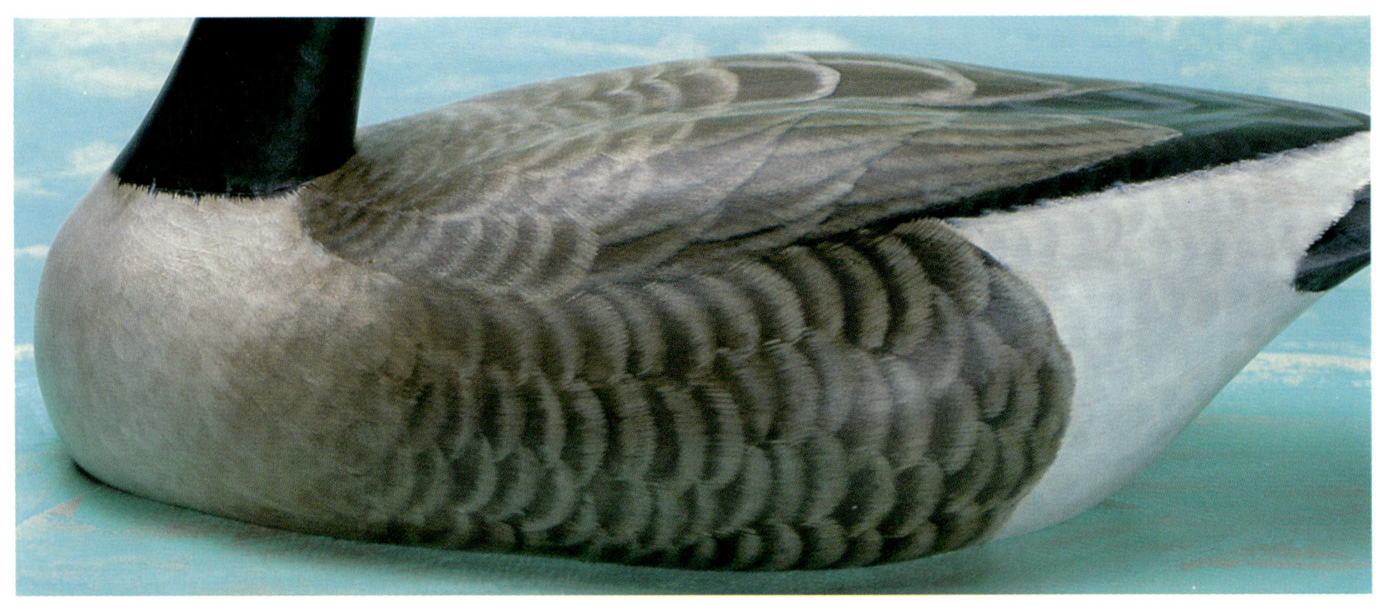

Detail - *Side Area*
   Refer to this close-up photograph for stroking on feathers on side area of the Canada Goose. Note the layers of wash on the breast area.

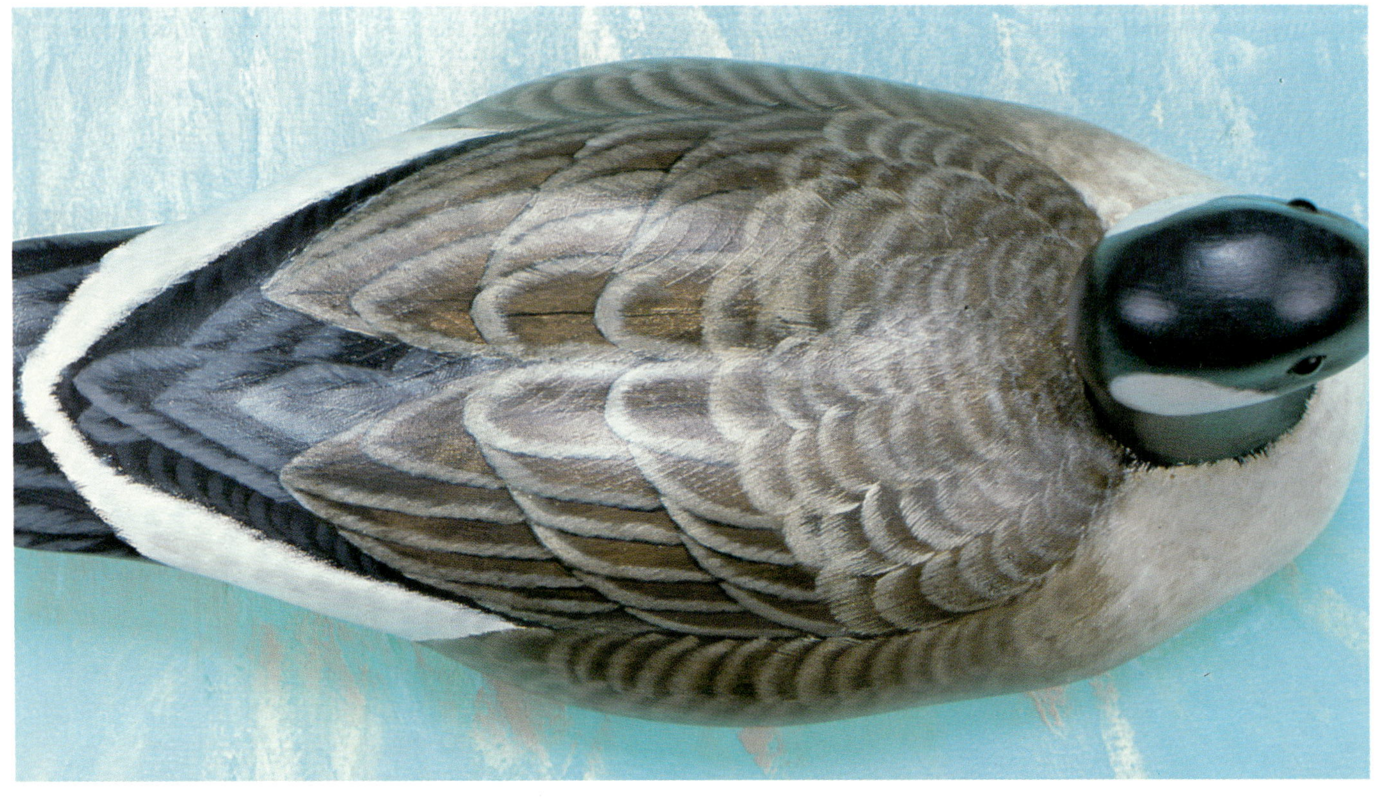

Detail - *Back Area*
   The feather arc on the sides and shoulders of geese is much shallower than on other waterfowl.

SNOW GOOSE

There are two species of Snow Geese in North America, the Greater Snow Goose along the eastern seaboard and the Lesser Snow Goose along the west coast and interior flyways.

The Snow Goose and the Blue Goose are the same species; they simply represent different color phases. Most of the species of wild geese in North America have many of the same habits and characteristics. The flying characteristics of Snow Geese are much more eratic than other species of geese. When disturbed, they tend to mill around in a confused state longer than Canadas. Their flight skeins are not as disciplined.

They are handsome birds with pink bills and feet whether they are the white phase or the blue phase. The reddish-orange that is sometimes found on the cheeks is usually caused by their diet and the minerals in the water where they feed.

In the winter , enormous flocks of Greater Snows are concentrated along the east coast tidal waters. The rice fields of Louisiana and Texas and the interior valleys of California also host great numbers of the Lesser Snows and Blues.

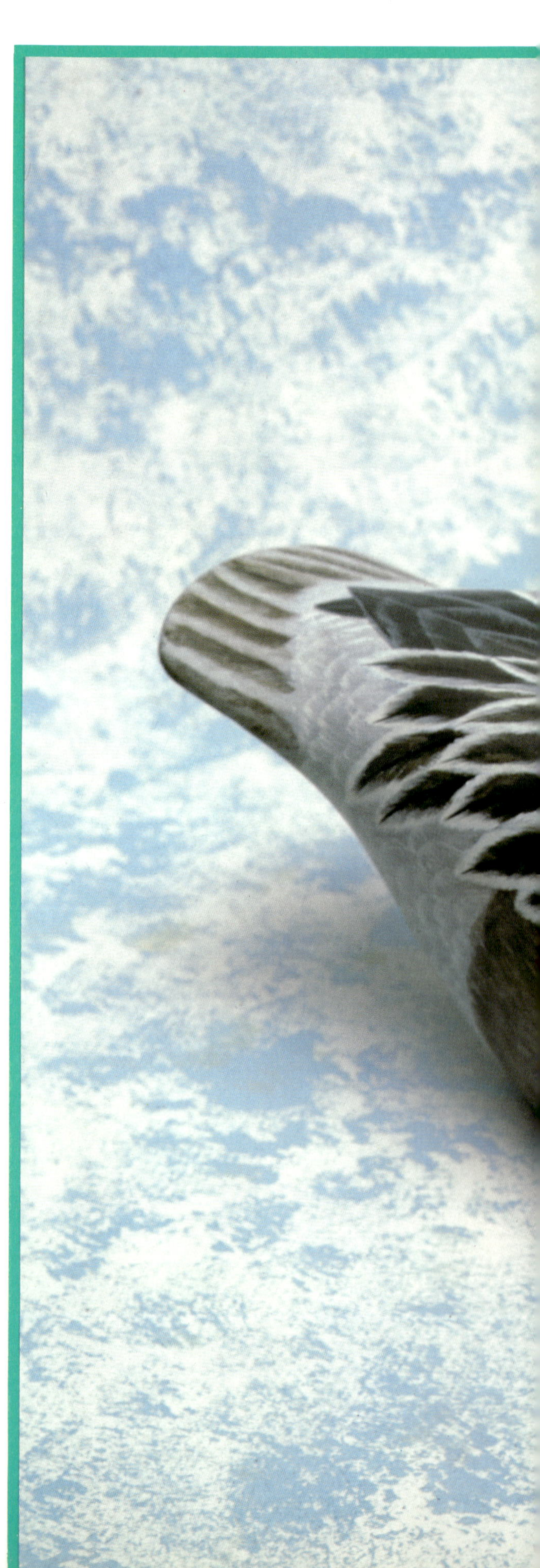

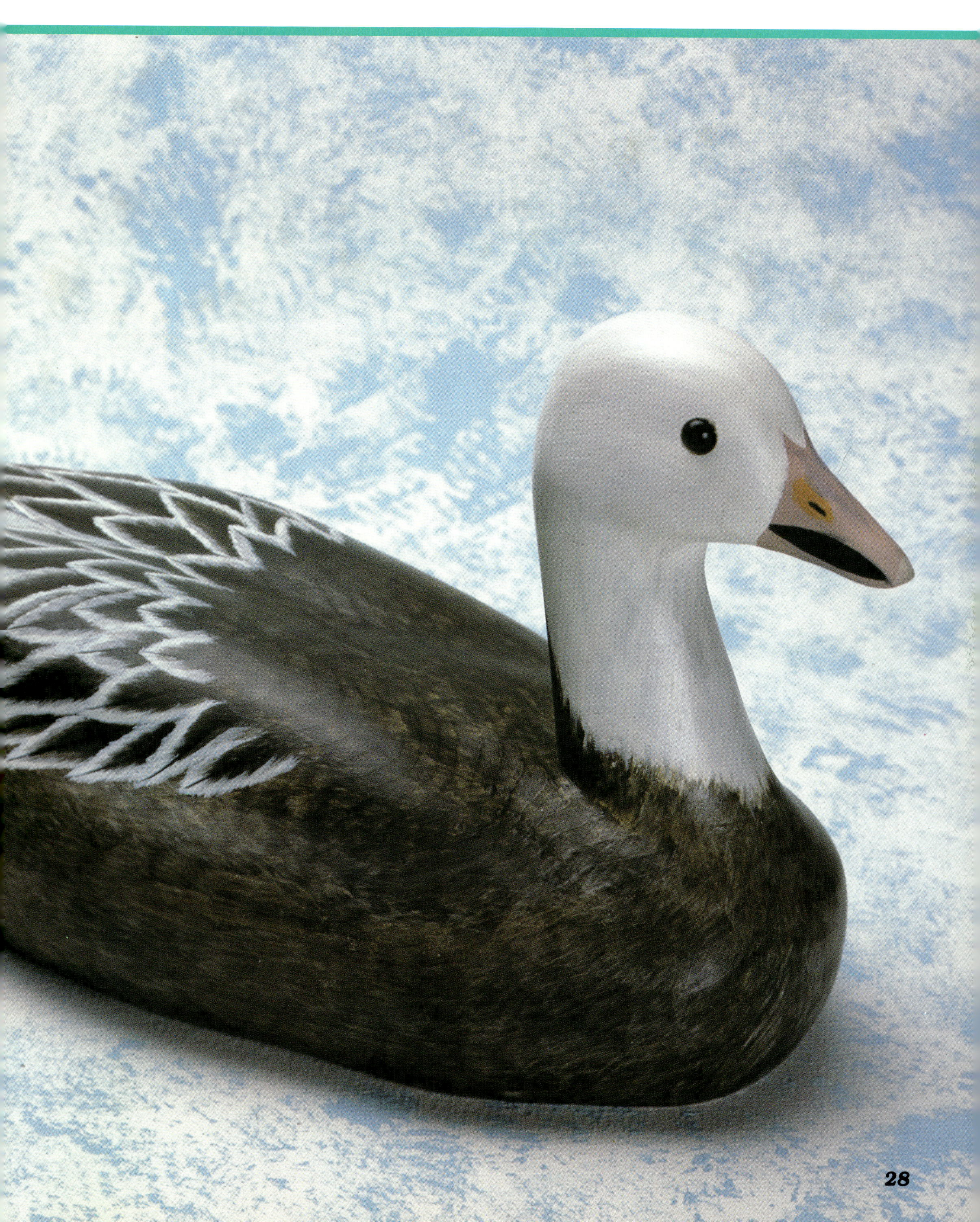

Permalba Colors

Raw Umber
Unbleached Titanium
Ivory Black
Cadmium Red Medium
Cadmium Orange
Titanium White

Brushes

Beebe Hopper Kats Tongue #12
Beebe Hopper Shader #10
Beebe Hopper Liner #0
Langnickel Kats Tongue #18

Sand decoy blank smooth, apply a wood sealer to decoy and let dry. When sealed, add a prime coat of paint. I prefer Permalba Titanium White acrylic. Let dry and sand lightly to create smooth surface.

Draw in abstract areas to be painted using Illustration #18 as a guide.

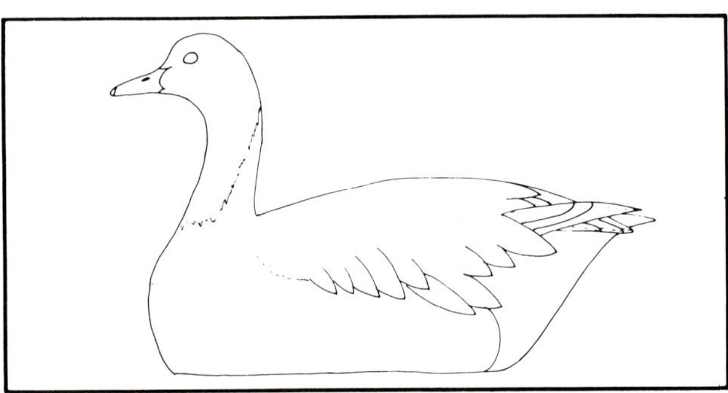

Illustration #18
Color placement diagram (Side view). Follow diagram to outline areas of color.

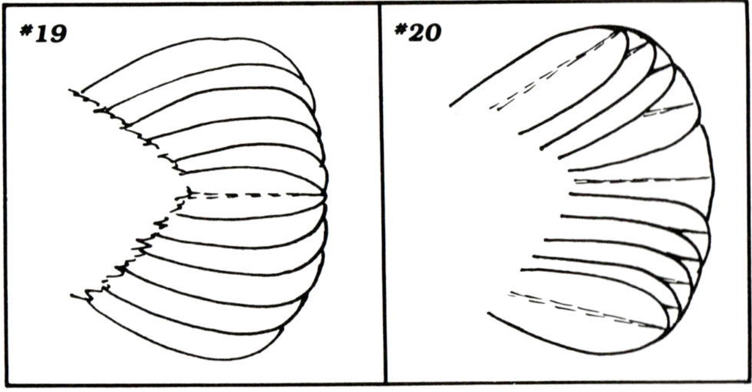

Illustration #19
Feather placement diagram (Top view). Follow diagram for general placement of featherstrokes for tail section.

Illustration #20
Feather placement diagram (Bottom view). Follow diagram for general placement of featherstrokes for tail section.

RUMP

Paint with very light gray mixed from White, Unbleached Titanium and a touch of Black. Paint on feather pattern in lighter gray using the Langnickel Kats Tongue #18 brush. Wash with lighter gray color. Repeat procedure until desired degree of softness is achieved.

TAIL

Paint tail section with a mix of Raw Umber and a small amount of Unbleached Titanium to lighten. Draw on feather pattern using black paint with the Beebe Hopper Liner #0. See Illustrations #19 and #20. Shade each feather inward from outer edge with light gray made with Black and Unbleached Titanium. Wash with Raw Umber. Highlight again with light gray.

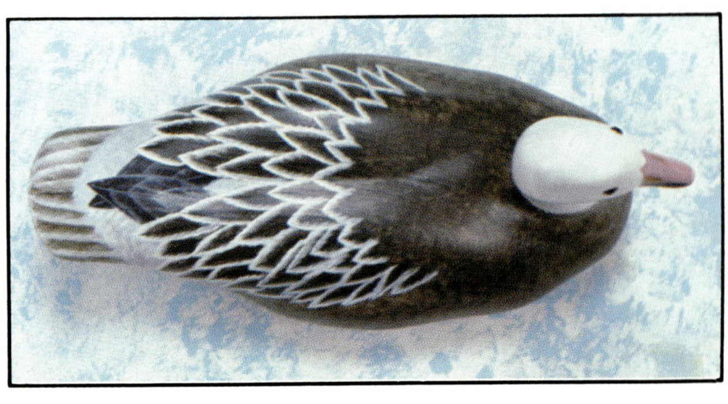

PRIMARIES

Paint primary section with Black. Draw in feather outlines using the Beebe Hopper Liner #0. Refer to Illustration #21. Shade inward from outer edge with very dark gray mixed from Black, White and Unbleached Titanium using the Beebe Hopper Shader #10.

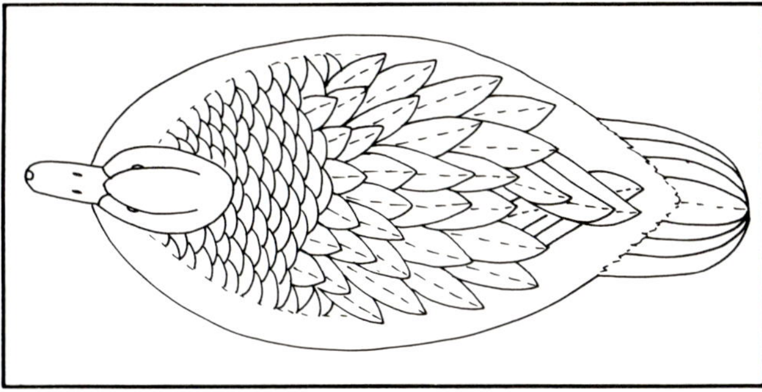

Illustration #21
Feather placement diagram (Top view). Follow diagram for general placement of featherstrokes for primaries.

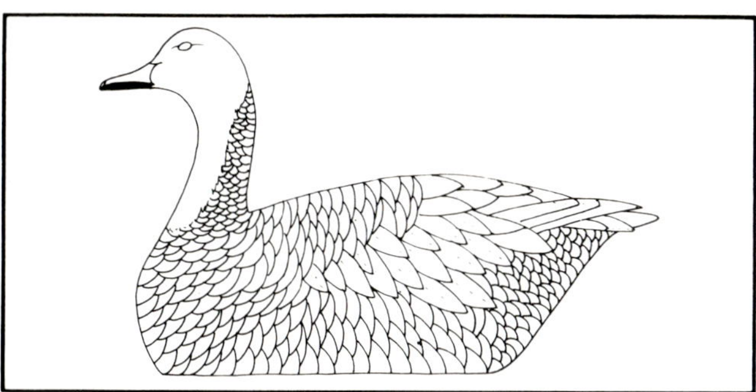

Illustration #22
Feather placement diagram (Side view). Follow diagram for general placement of featherstrokes for neck, wing and tail areas.

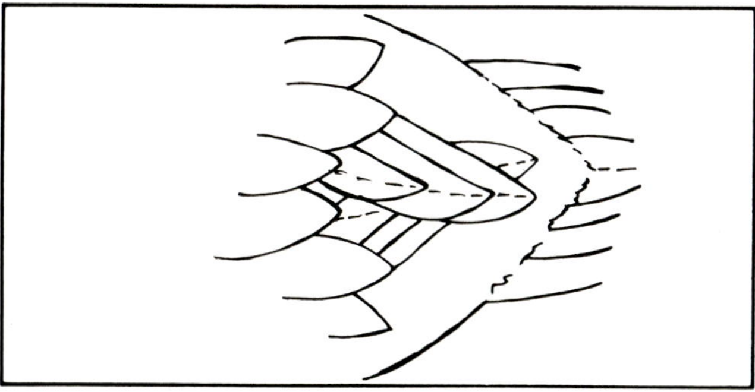

Illustration #23
Feather placement diagram (Top view). Follow diagram for general placement of featherstrokes on primary and tail sections.

BODY

Paint back, sides, chest and back of neck with Raw Umber. Blend dark area into light area at neckline to avoid a hard line. Draw in elongated feather pattern of lower back with the Beebe Hopper Liner #0, using Illustrations #22 and #23 for feather layout pattern. Shade elongated feathers from outer edge inward using pale gray mixed from Titanium White, Black and Unbleached Titanium. Use the Langnickel Kats Tongue #18 fanned to maximum and Unbleached Titanium to paint feather pattern over upper back and sides. Use the Beebe Hopper Kats Tongue #12 for smaller feathers of breast and back of neck. See Illustrations #22 and #23 for feather layout. Wash with Raw Umber. Repeat procedure until desired softness is achieved.

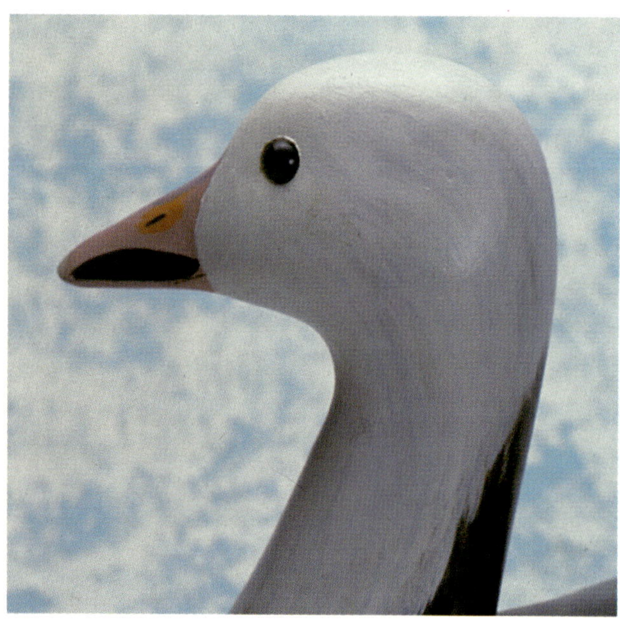

HEAD

Mix Titanium White and a touch of Unbleached Titanium to eliminate chalky appearance of white. Paint head and front of neck keeping paint smooth and even.

BILL

A pink mixed from Cadmium Red Medium, Unbleached Titanium and a touch of dark Orange near to nostril. The "grin" patch is Black.

EYE

Brown

SNOW GOOSE/BLUE PHASE

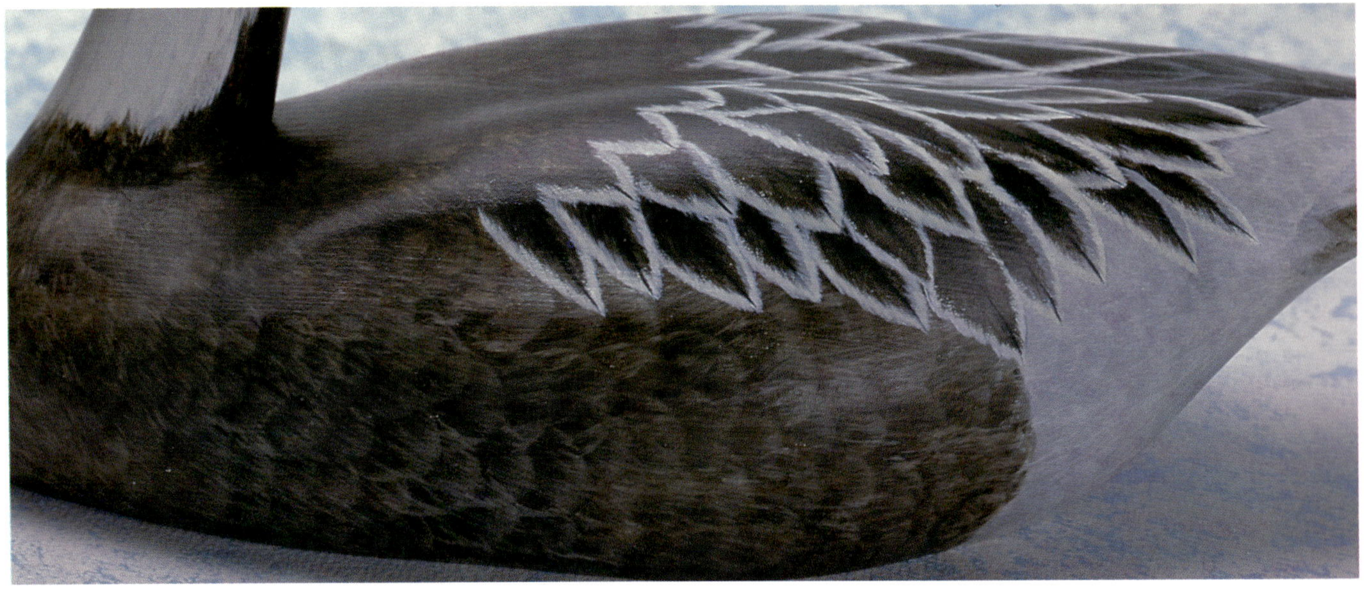

Detail - Side Area

Refer to this close-up photograph for stroking on feathers on the side area of the Snow Goose/Blue Phase. Note the distinct feather sections.

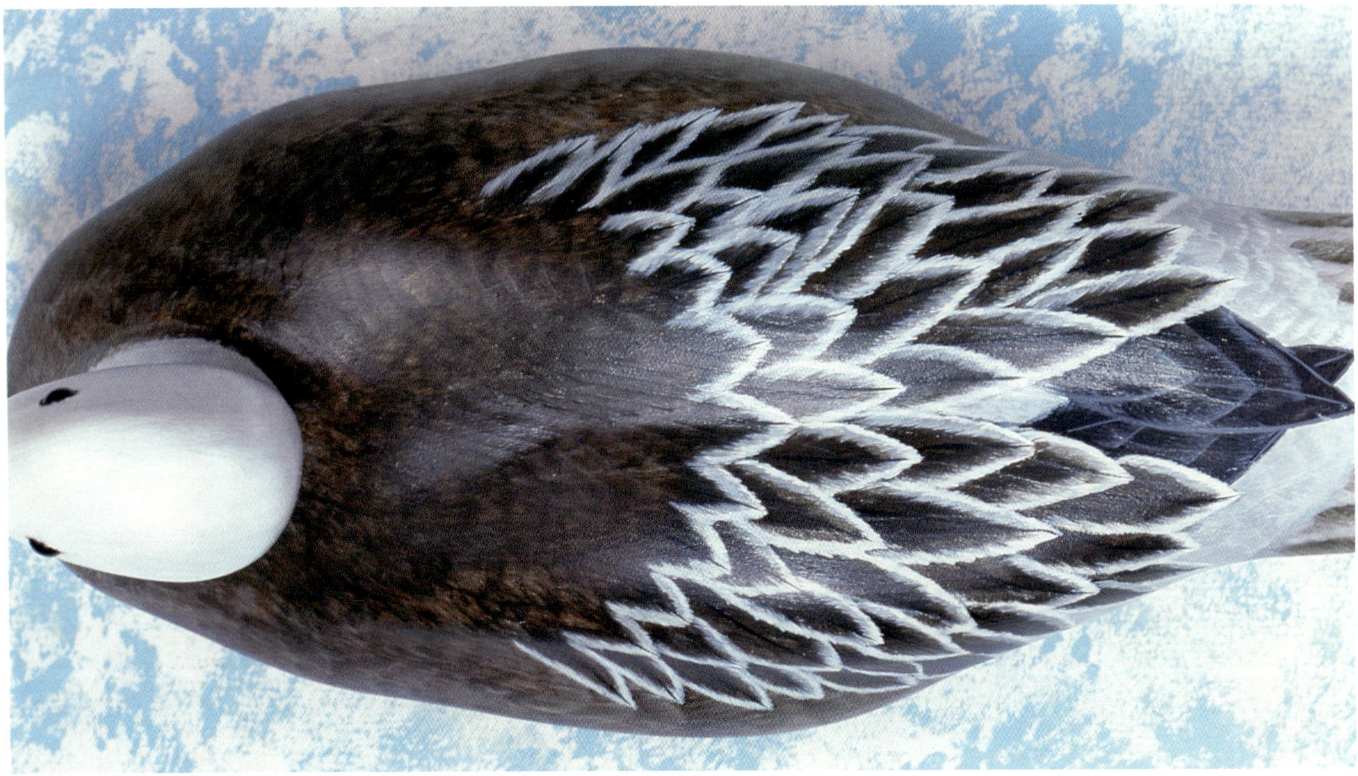

Detail - Back Area

The feather pattern on the back area of the Snow Goose/Blue Phase is created through distinct and separate feather pattern groups.

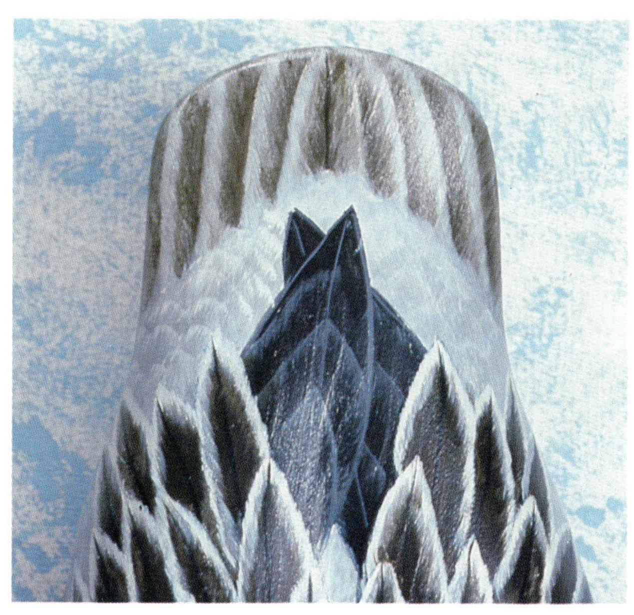

Detail - *Tail Area*
   The large square tail area is beautiful with a contrast from black to bright white.

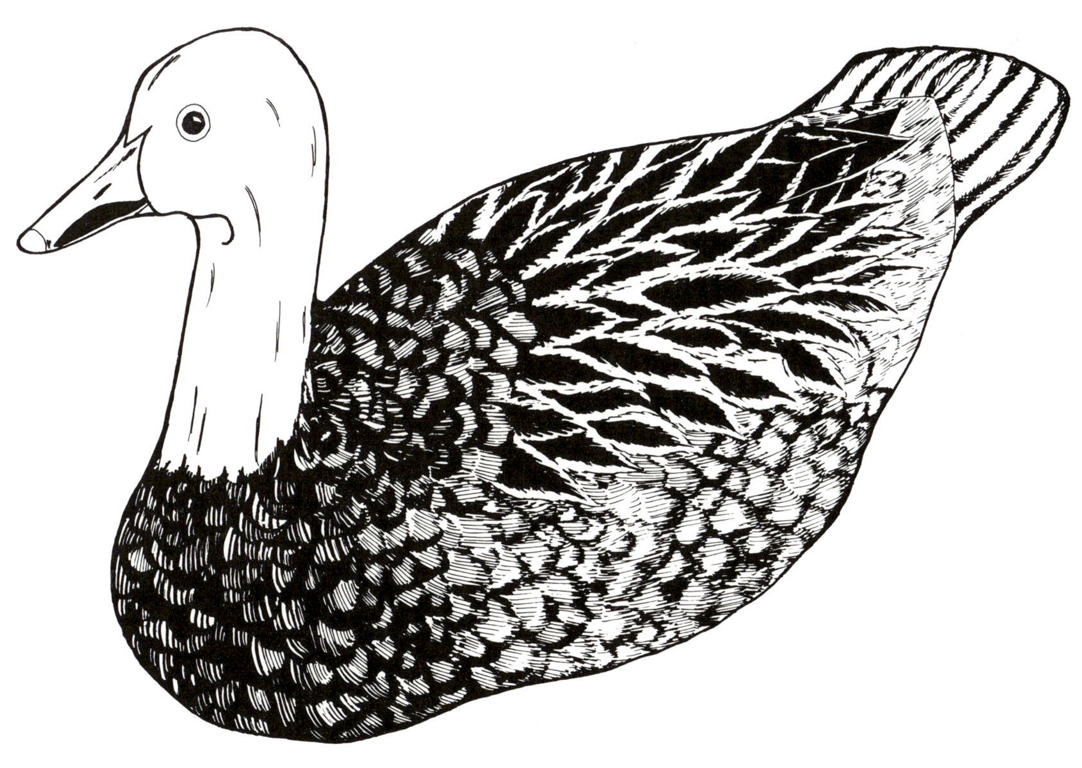

SNOW GOOSE

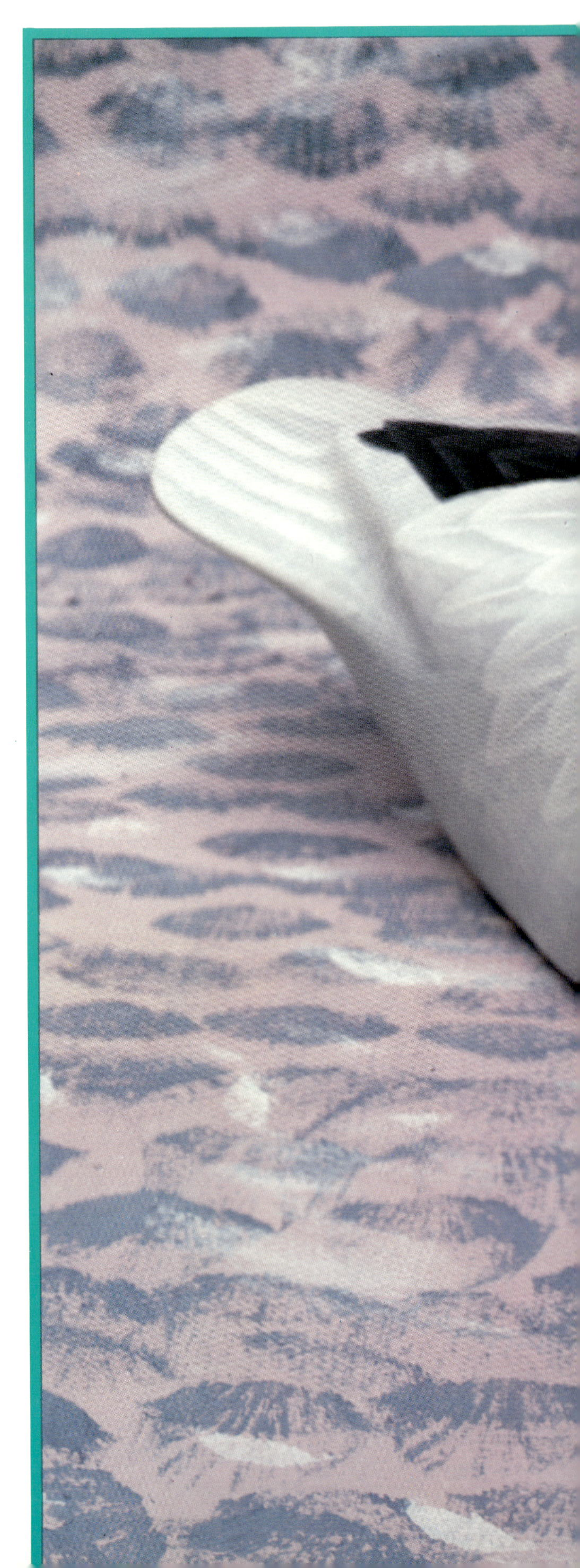

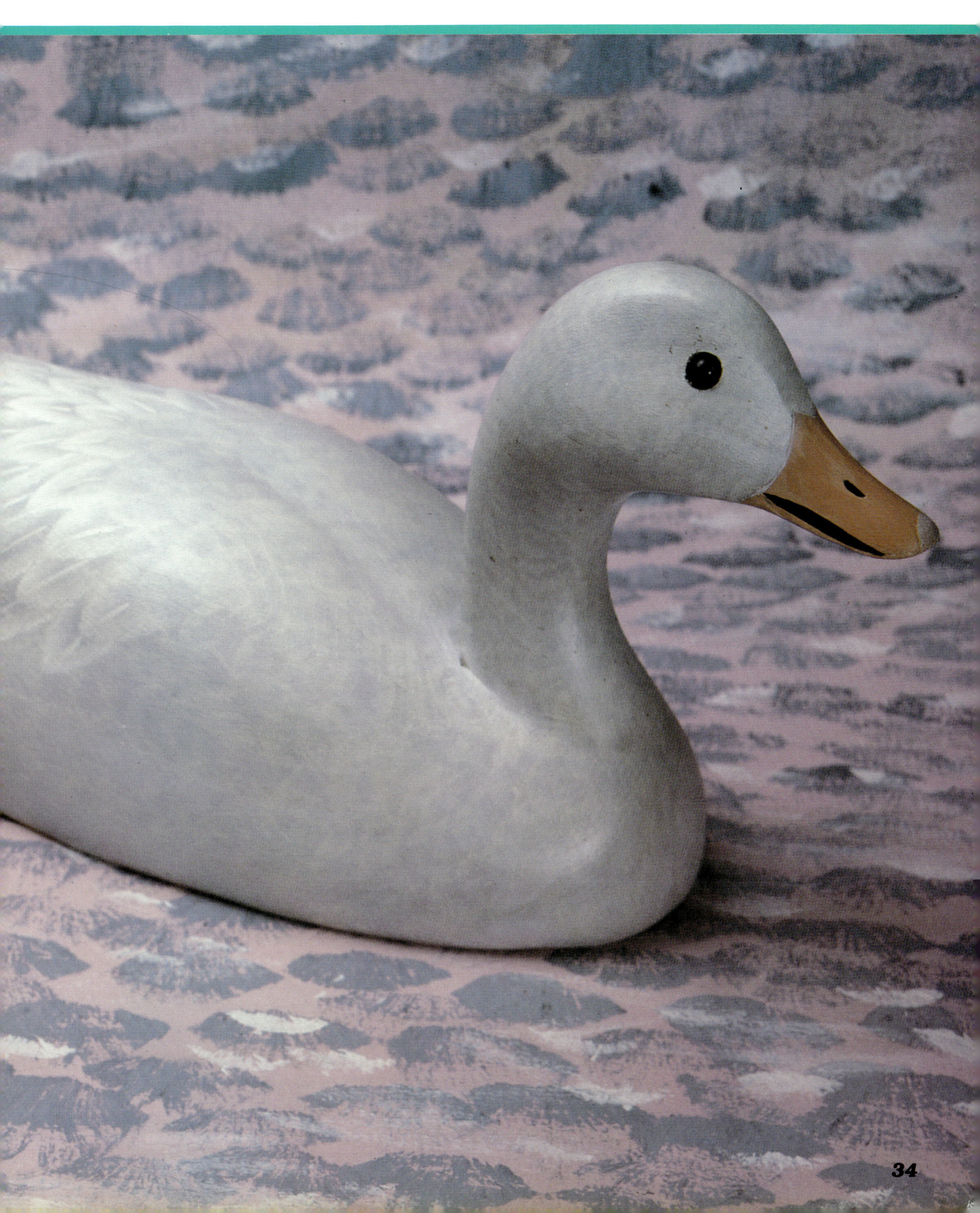

SNOW GOOSE

Permalba Colors

Titanium White
Ivory Black
Unbleached Titanium
Paynes Gray
Cadmium Red Medium
Cadmium Orange

Brushes

Beebe Hopper Liner #0
Beebe Hopper Shader #10
Beebe Hopper Kats Tongue #12
Langnickel Kats Tongue #18

Titanium White + Paynes Gray = Color mixture.

Illustration #24
Shown above are the color chips to create the mixture used to base the entire body of the Snow Goose, white phase. Titanium White is added to Paynes Gray to acheive a light bluish gray.

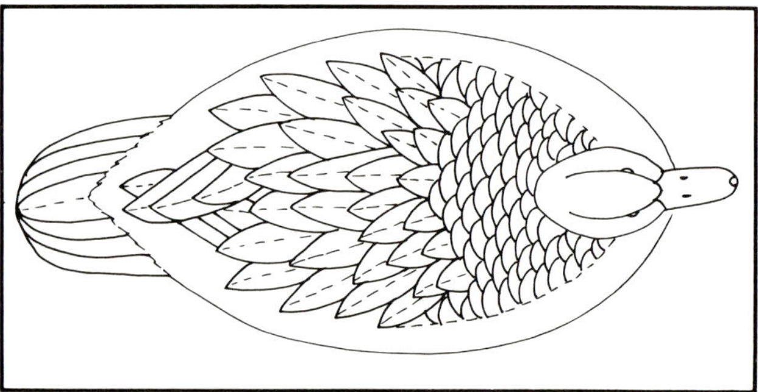

Illustration #25
Feather placement diagram (Top view). Follow diagram general placement of featherstrokes on primary and tail sections.

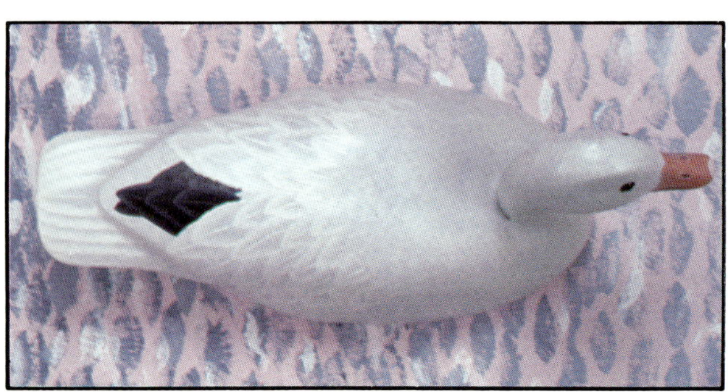

Sand decoy smooth. Apply a wood sealer to decoy and let dry. Paint whole decoy with a mixture of Titanium White and Paynes Gray to make a light bluish gray, being careful to keep the paint smooth and even. See Illustration #24. The Snow Goose is a truly white bird that has black wingtips. In order to paint this decoy successfully, it will be a matter of shading the feathers to create a "white on white" effect. The blue gray base will act as a shadow color to help create the dimensional look.

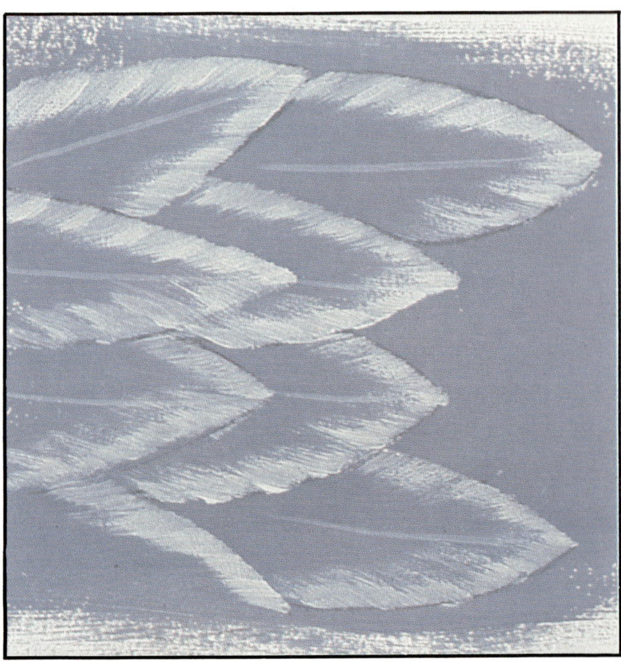

Illustration #26
Feathers are shaded from outside edge using a mixture of Titanium White and Unbleached Titanium.

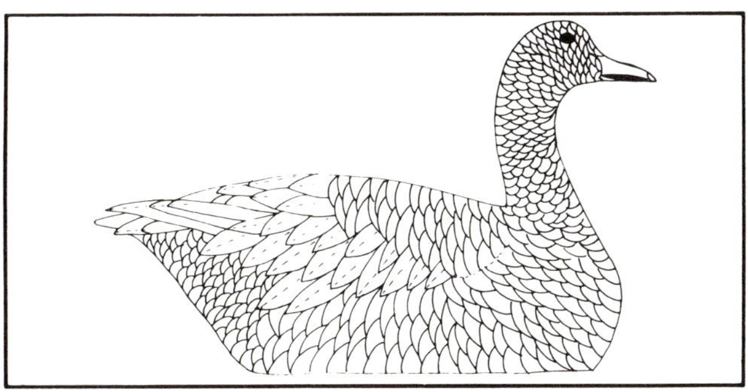

Illustration #27

Feather placement diagram (Side view). Follow diagram for general placement of featherstrokes on head, neck, wing and tail areas.

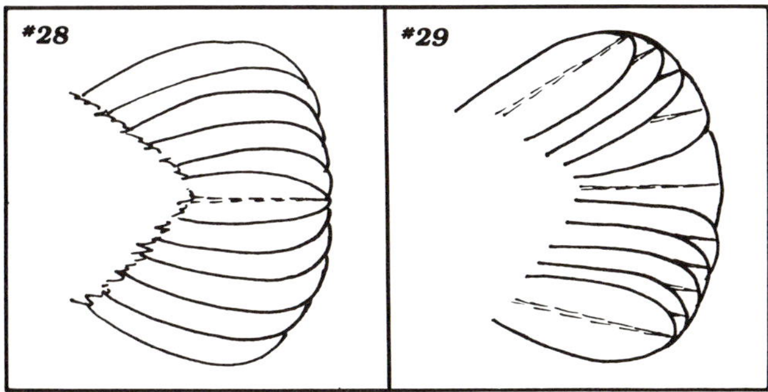

Illustration #28

Feather placement diagram (Top view). Follow diagram for general placement of featherstrokes for tail section.

Illustration #29

Feather placement diagram (Bottom view). Follow diagram for general placement of featherstrokes for tail section.

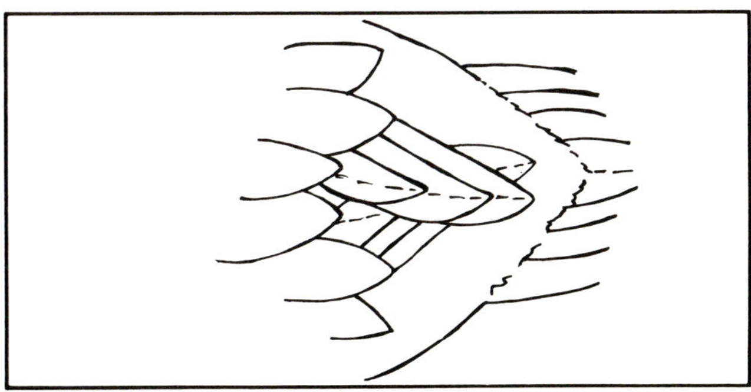

Illustration #30

Feather placement diagram (Top view). Follow diagram for general placement of featherstrokes on primaries.

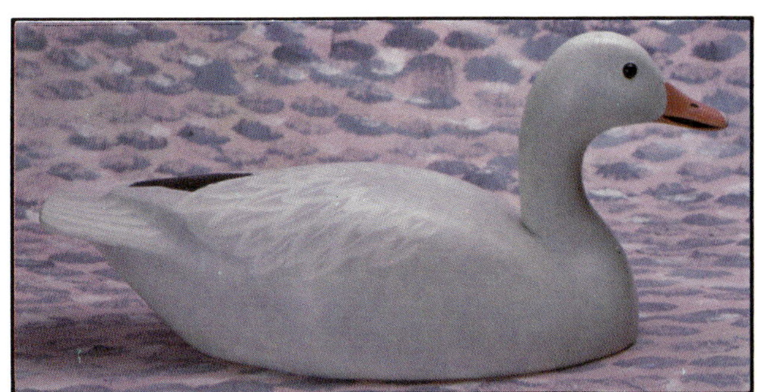

Lightly draw in the elongated feather pattern on the lower back with Beebe Hopper Liner #0 and very light gray paint. See Illustration #25 for feather layout. Using Titanium White and a touch of Unbleached Titanium, shade elongated feathers inward from outside edge using the Beebe Hopper Shader #10. See Illustration #26.

To create mixture for feather pattern, mix white with a touch of Unbleached Titanium. For head and chest use the Beebe Hopper Kats Tongue #12; for back and sides use Langnickel Kats Tongue #18. Paint the feather pattern over the whole body excluding elongated feathers. See Illustration #27 for feather layout. Apply a thin wash of the white mix over the whole body. Continue layers of feather patterns and washes until desired softness is acquired.

TAIL

Using feather layout, Illustrations #28 and #29, draw in feathers with pale gray. Shade from outer edge inward using the white mix with the Beebe Hopper Shader #10.

PRIMARIES

Paint primary area with Black. Using feather layout pattern, draw in feather pattern with dark gray with the Beebe Hopper Liner #0. See Illustration #30. Shade from outer edge inward with dark gray made from Titanium White and Paynes Gray using the Beebe Hopper Shader #10.

BILL

Use Cadmium Red Medium, Unbleached Titanium and a touch of Cadmium Orange for pink color. "Grin" patch is black. Nail is off white.

EYE

Brown

SNOW GOOSE

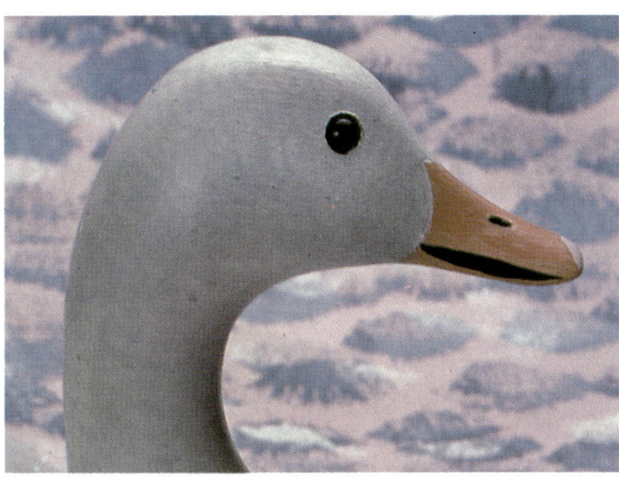

Detail - *Head Area*
The head area of the Snow Goose is painted in subtle shades of gray, highlighted with Unbleached Titanium.

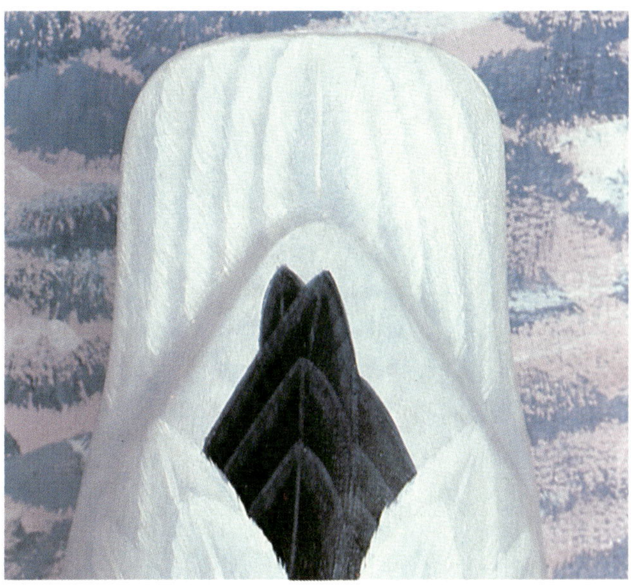

Detail - *Tail Area*
Take note of the stroke direction of the feathers in the tail area. These feathers are kept very light in value on the tips.

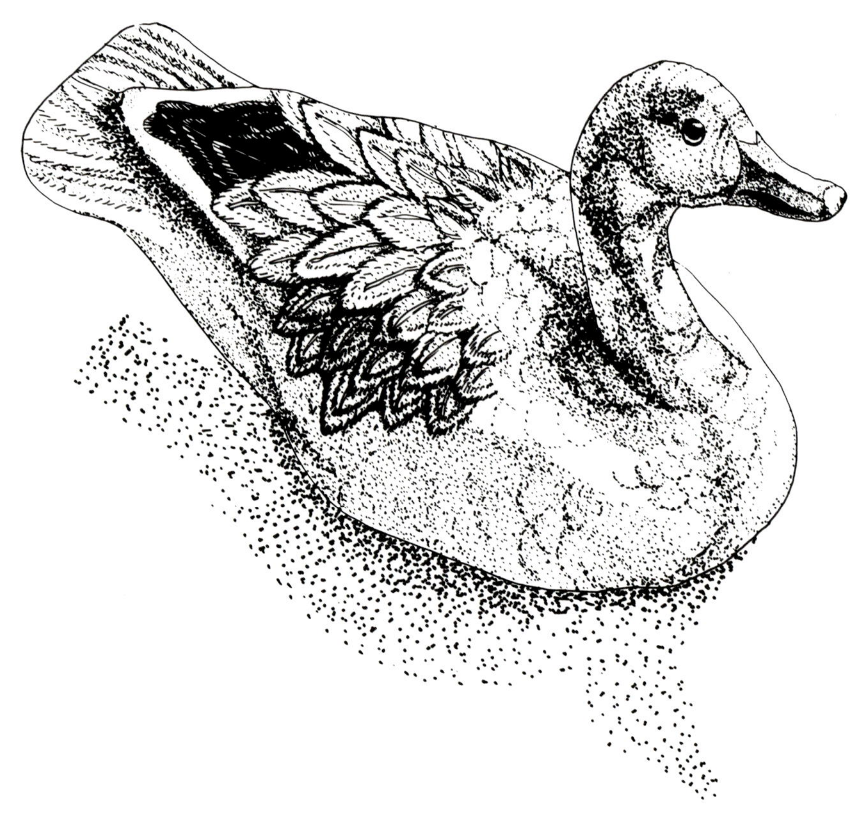

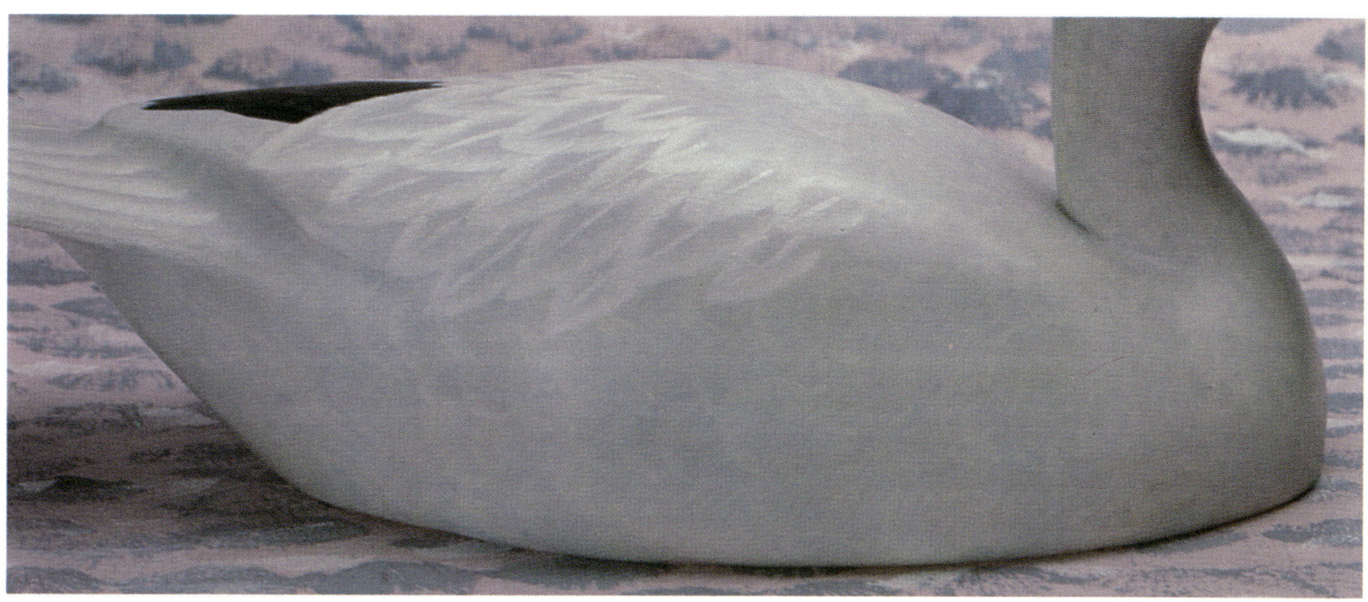

Detail - *Side Area*
    Refer to this close-up photograph for stroking on feathers on the side area of the Snow Goose. The feathers are created with continued layers of feather patterns and washes.

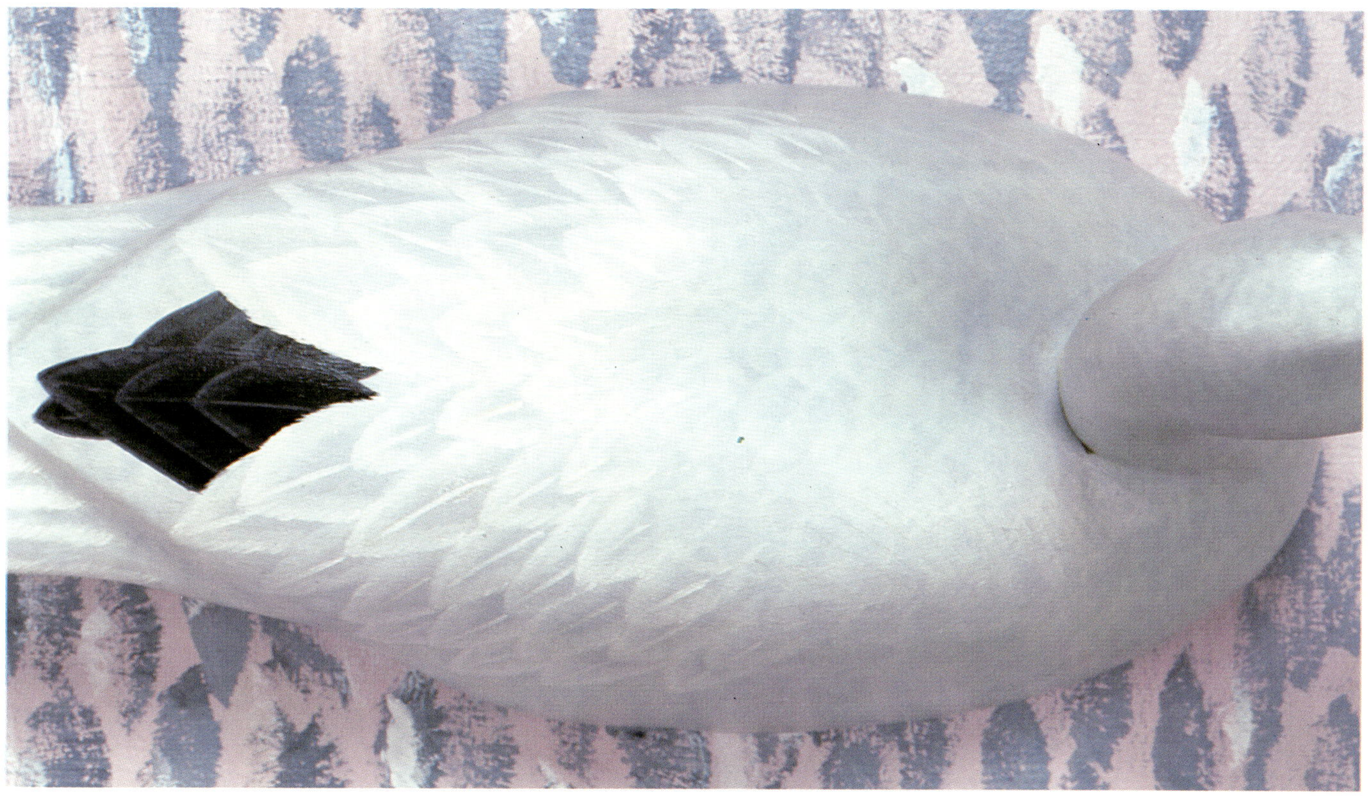

Detail - *Back Area*
    The feather pattern on the back of the Snow Goose is created partially through the application of washes and partially through featherstrokes.

WHITE-FRONTED GOOSE

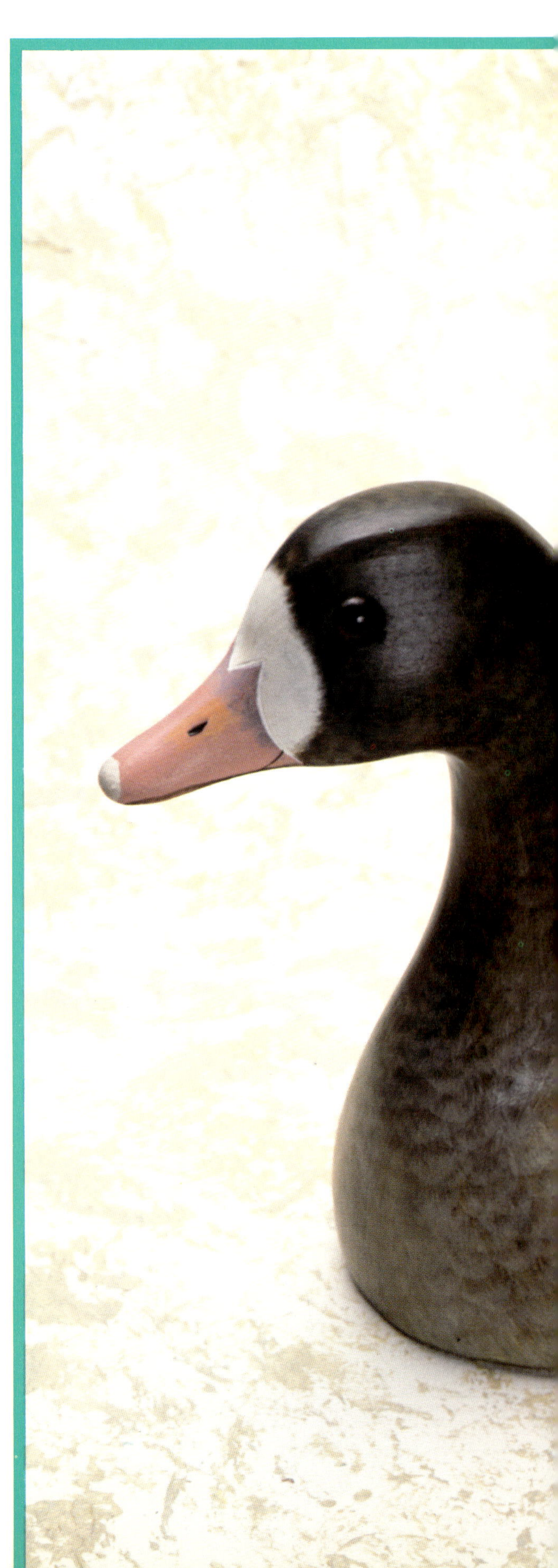

The White-Fronted Goose is named so because of the white forehead, not because it has a white breast or front. They are easily distinguished among flocks of feeding Canada Geese by the fact that they are grayish with black splotches on the breast and belly and they have a pink bill and orange colored legs and feet. The black splotches on the under side result in the common name of "speckle belly".

They are rare along the Eastern seaboard, but are more prevalent in the midwest and are abundant along the Pacific Coast.

They, like the Canada Goose, are monogamous and usually form the bond of permanency during their second year.

Primarily, White-Fronted Geese are vegetarians and many farmers' grain fields have been decimated by these wild and wonderful birds.

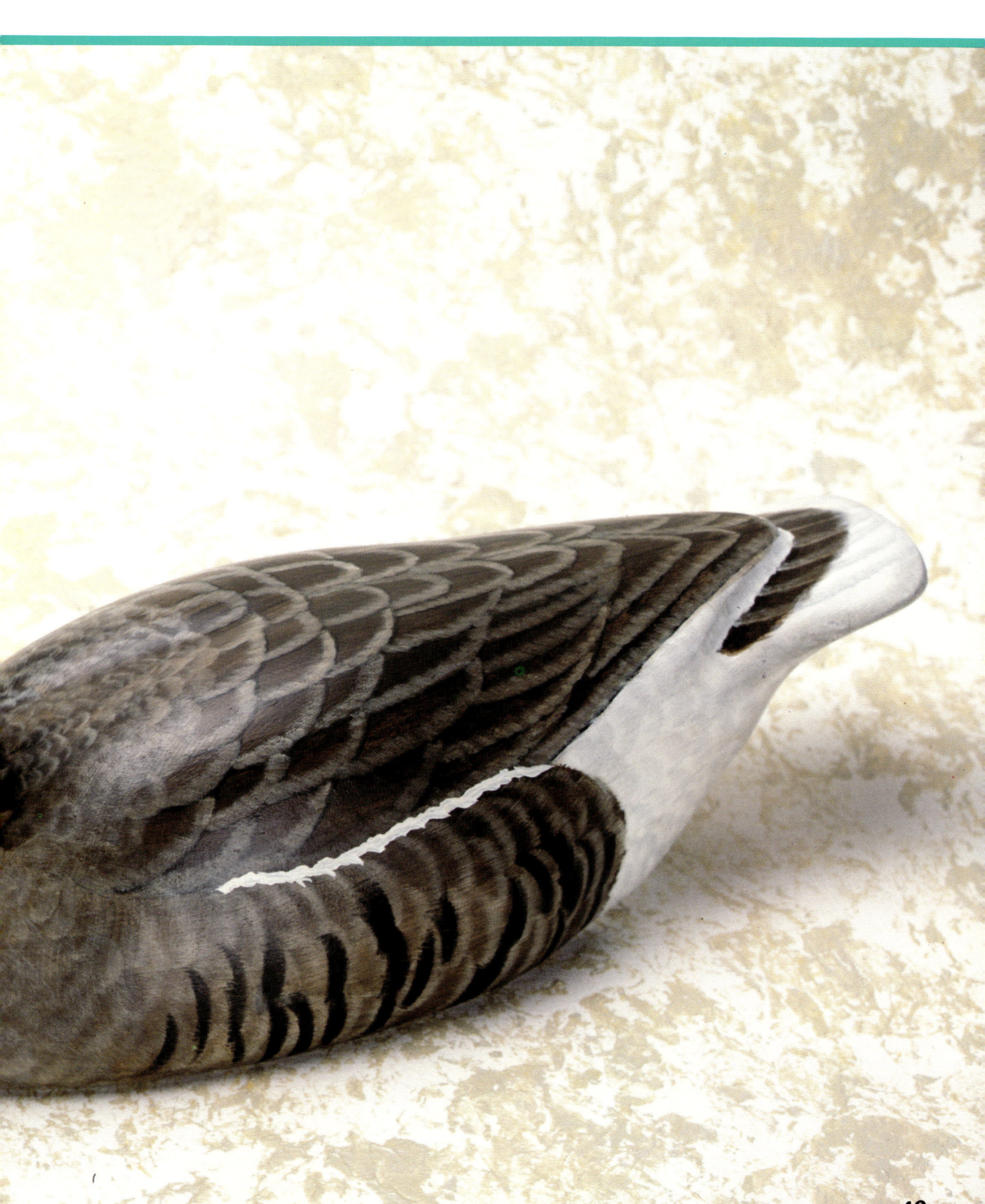

WHITE-FRONTED GOOSE

Permalba Colors

Raw Umber
Ivory Black
Titanium White
Unbleached Titanium
Cadmium Red Medium
Cadmium Red Deep

Brushes

Langnickel Kats Tongue #18
Beebe Hopper Kats Tongue #12
Beebe Hopper Liner #0
Beebe Hopper Shader #10

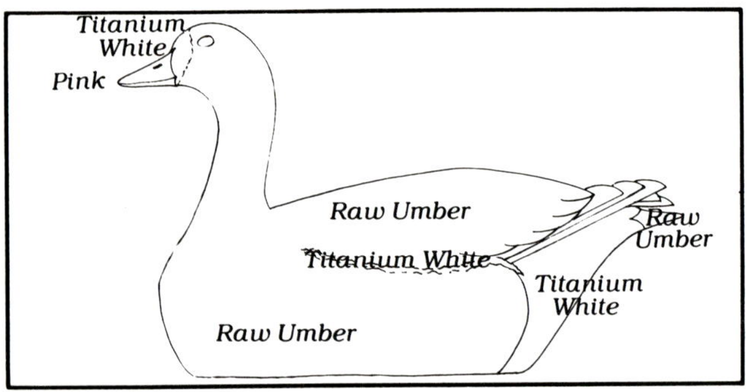

Illustration #31

Color placement diagram (Side view). Follow diagram to outline areas of color.

Before beginning to paint the White-Fronted Goose, you should sand the decoy to ensure that it is smooth. Then apply a wood sealer to the entire decoy and let dry. After the sealer is dry, apply a prime coat of paint. When dry, lightly sand again.

Draw in abstract areas to be painted using Illustration #31 as a guide.

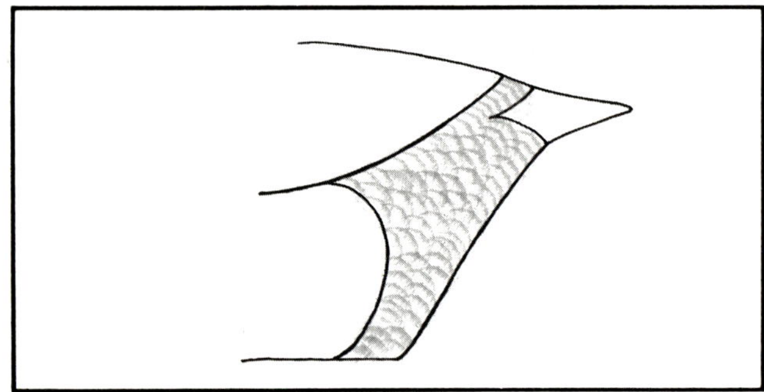

Illustration #34

Refer to the contour of feather placement for rump area of White-Fronted Goose.

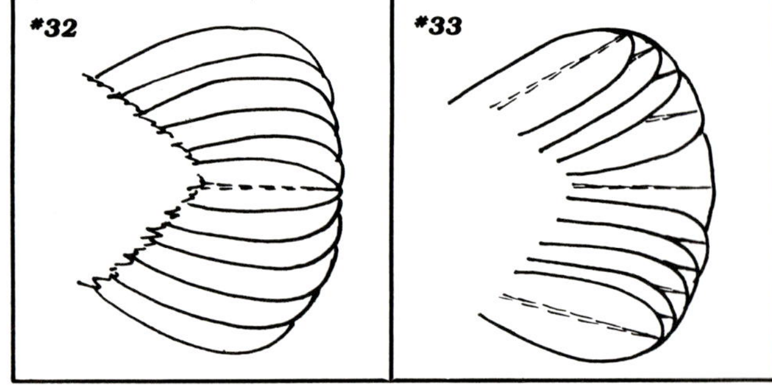

Illustration #32

Feather placement diagram (Top view). Follow diagram for general placement of featherstrokes for tail section.

Illustration #33

Feather placement diagram (Bottom view). Follow diagram for general placement of featherstrokes for tail section.

TAIL

Paint the tail section with Raw Umber. Draw in feather pattern with white using Illustrations # 32 and # 33 as a guide. Shade each feather with the Beebe Hopper Shader #10 inward from outer edge using a mix of Titanium White and a touch of Unbleached Titanium. A light touch and thin paint is necessary.

RUMP

Apply Titanium White with a touch of Unbleached Titanium to both upper and lower rump. Be sure that paint is smooth and even. To create feather pattern, use Titanium White mixed with a small amount of Black to make a light gray. Using the Beebe Hopper Kats Tongue #12, make a feather pattern over the area following the contour of feathers. If pattern is too harsh, apply a wash of the white mixture. Refer to Illustration #34.

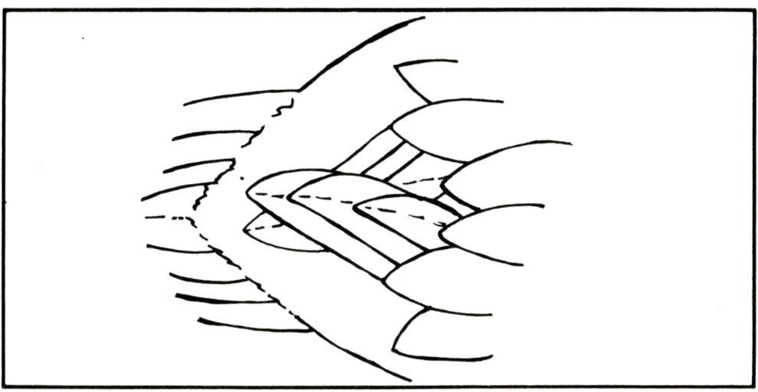

Illustration #35
Feather placement diagram (Top view). Follow diagram for general placement of featherstrokes for primaries.

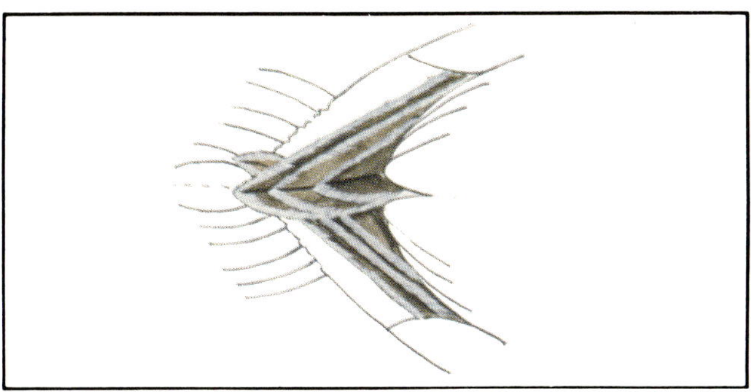

Illustration #36
Shade primaries inward with Titanium White mixed with a touch of Unbleached Titanium.

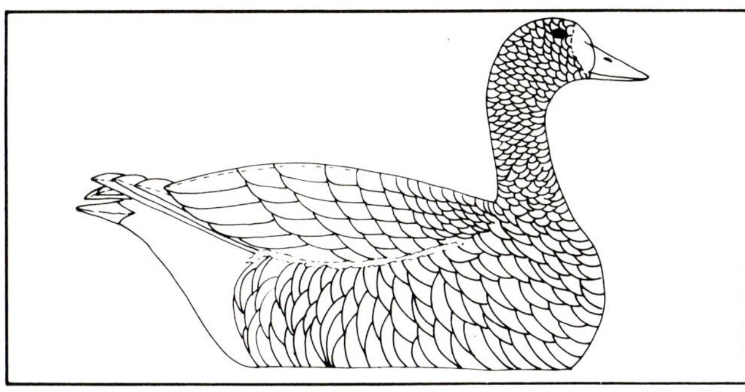

Illustration #37
Feather placement diagram (Side view). Follow diagram for general placement of featherstrokes on head, neck, wing and tail areas.

PRIMARIES

Paint primary section with Raw Umber mixed with a touch of black to make a dark brown. Draw in feather outline using the Beebe Hopper Liner #0 and black paint. Refer to Illustration #35. Shade inward from outer edge with a mix of Titanium White and a touch of

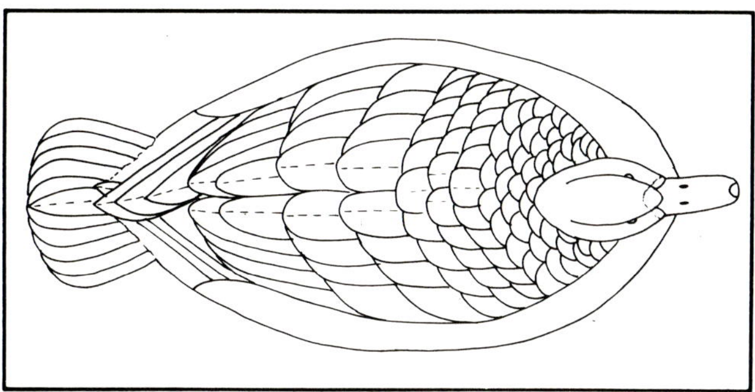

Illustration #38
Feather placement diagram (Top view). Follow diagram for general placement of featherstrokes on primary and tail sections.

Unbleached Titanium using the Beebe Hopper Shader #10. Refer to Illustration #36.

BODY

Paint back, sides, head and chest with Raw Umber. Referring to Illustrations #37 and #38, draw in feather pattern over entire body. The larger secondary feathers on lower back are shaded inward from outer edge using the Beebe Hopper Shader #10 with Unbleached Titanium. To paint the feather pattern of shoulders and head, use Unbleached Titanium with the Beebe Hopper Kats Tongue #12. For the sides, use Unbleached Titanium and the Langnickel Kats Tongue #18 fanned to maximum. When feather pattern is completed over the whole bird, apply a wash of Raw Umber over all dark areas. Repeat procedure until desired effect is achieved.

The white area along the side pocket is painted with the Beebe Hopper Liner #0 using Titanium White and a touch of Unbleached Titanium. The outer edge of the secondary feathers is given a final coat of the white mix with the Liner brush. Irregular feathers on chest and sides are painted with Black to form the "black splotches".

FOREHEAD

Titanium White with a touch of Unbleached Titanium.

BILL

Pink is made by mixing Cadmium Red Medium, Unbleached Titanium and a touch of Cadmium Orange. It is pale bluish at the base and yellow orange around nostril. Nail is off white.

EYE

Brown

WHITE-FRONTED GOOSE

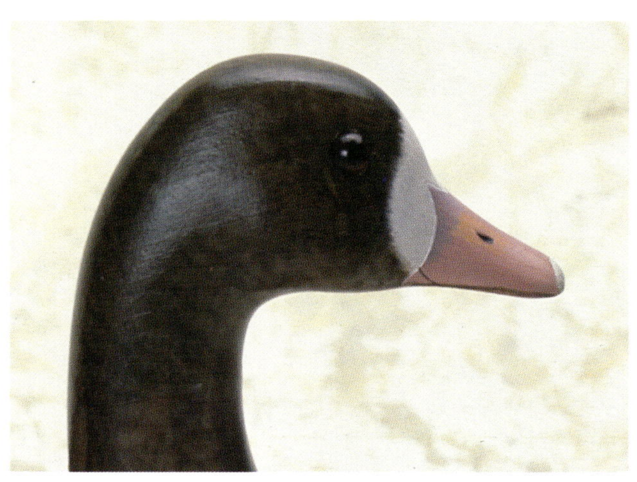

Detail - *Head Area*
The head area of the White-Fronted Goose is highlighted with delicate featherstrokes. Note the striking colors in the bill.

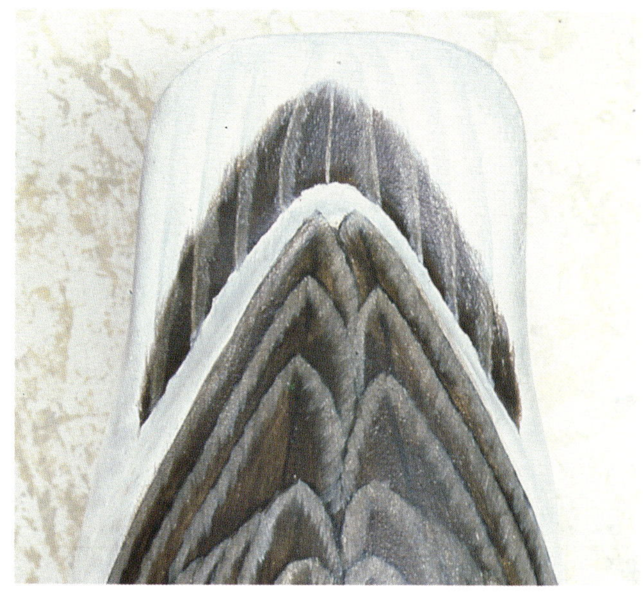

Detail - *Tail Area*
Take note of the stroke direction of the feathers in the tail area. The tip is kept lighter in color value.

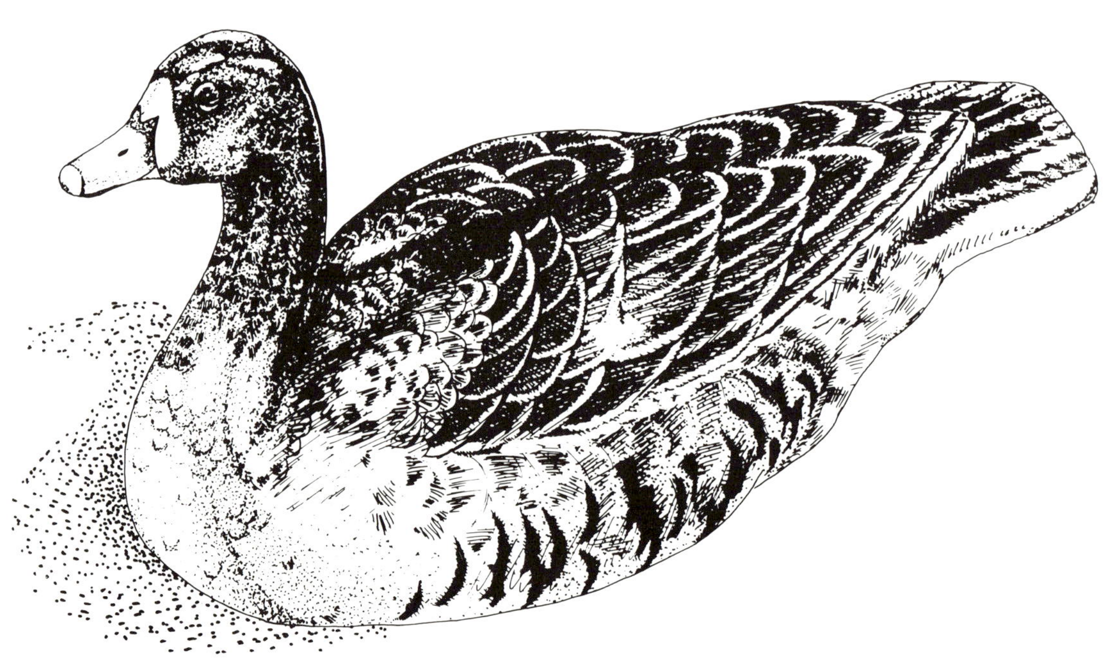

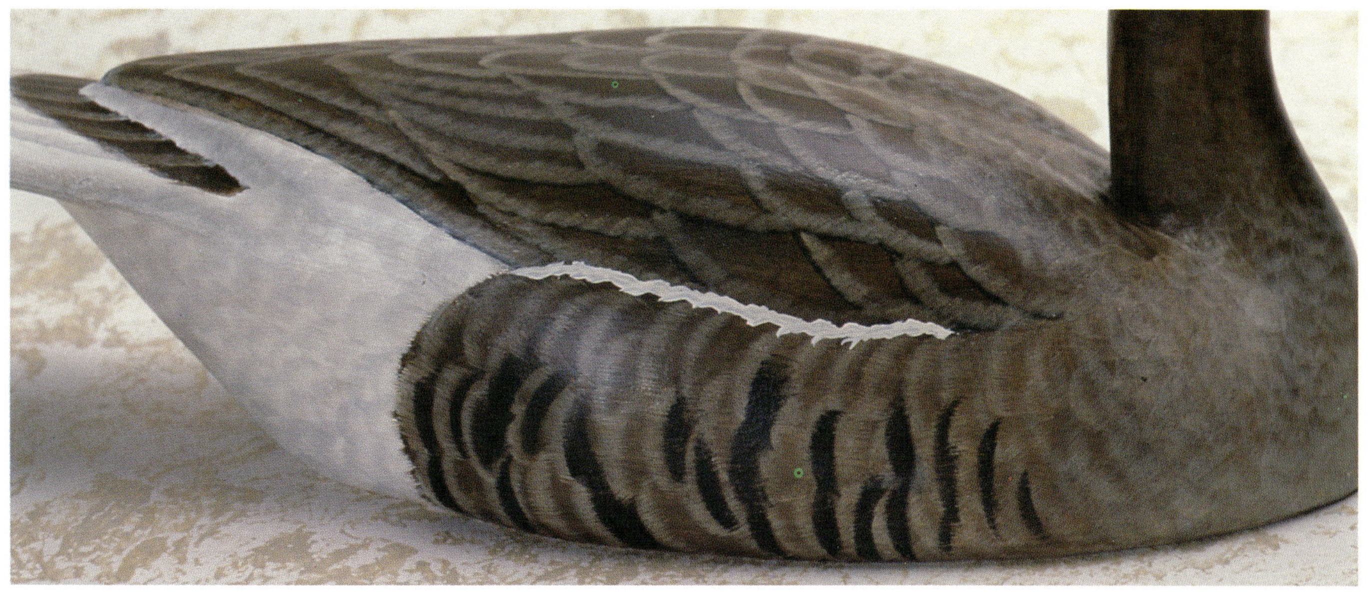

Detail - *Side Area*

Refer to this close-up photograph for stroking on feathers on the side area of the White–Fronted Goose. Note the "black splotches" painted on in an irregular pattern.

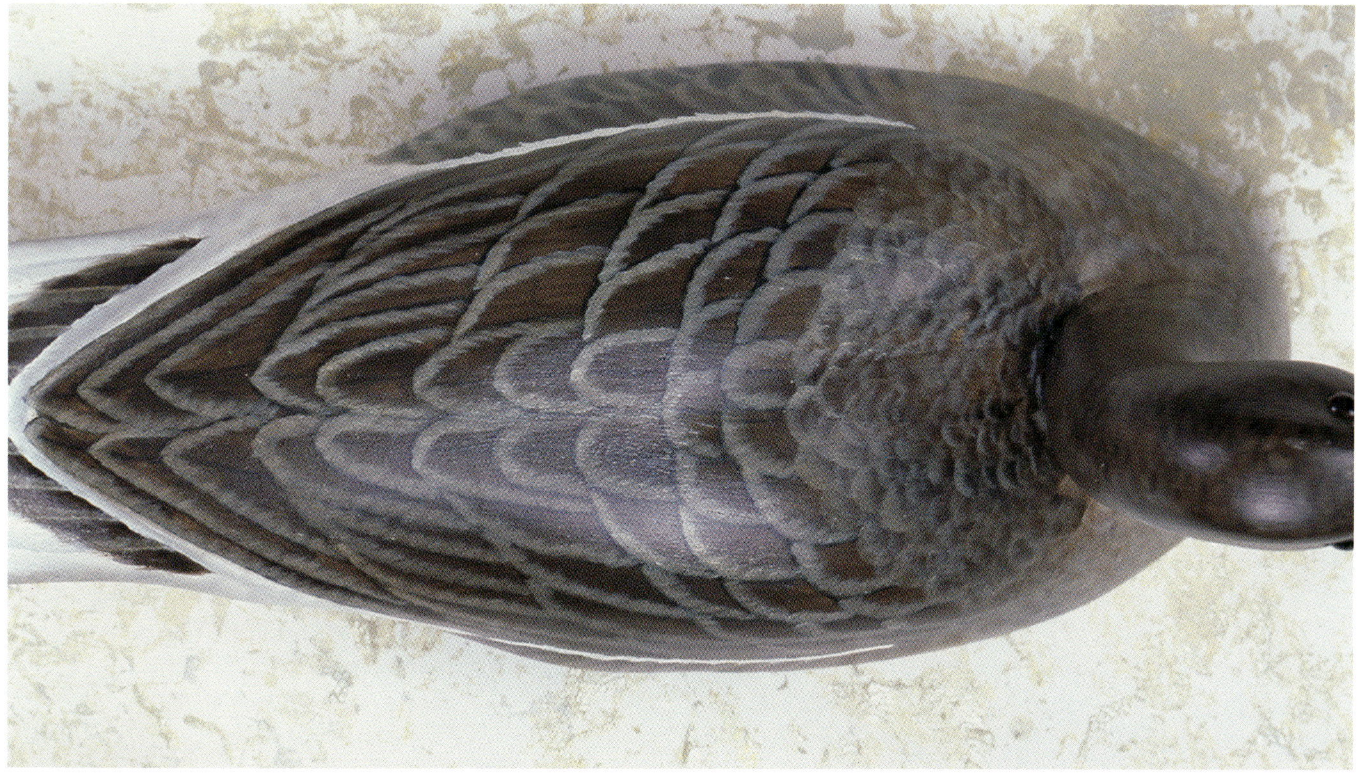

Detail - *Back Area*

The feather arc on the sides and shoulders of geese is much shallower than on other waterfowl.

EMPEROR GOOSE

The Emperor Goose is a strikingly beautiful species of sea goose which we are not often privileged to see in the wild. It is commonly referred to as a "Bean Goose". The range of this goose is from coastal Alaska, to coastal Siberia and Arctic Canada. During the winter, a few make their way down the Pacific Coast and into California. The silver gray of the feathers that are highlighted and edged with white and black make a dramatic feather pattern, along with a multi-colored red bill and yellow feet and legs.

Mostly vegetarian, they do eat some crustaceans, mollusks and similar sea life.

Although statistics are few, it is thought that Emperor Geese are strongly bonded and mate for life.

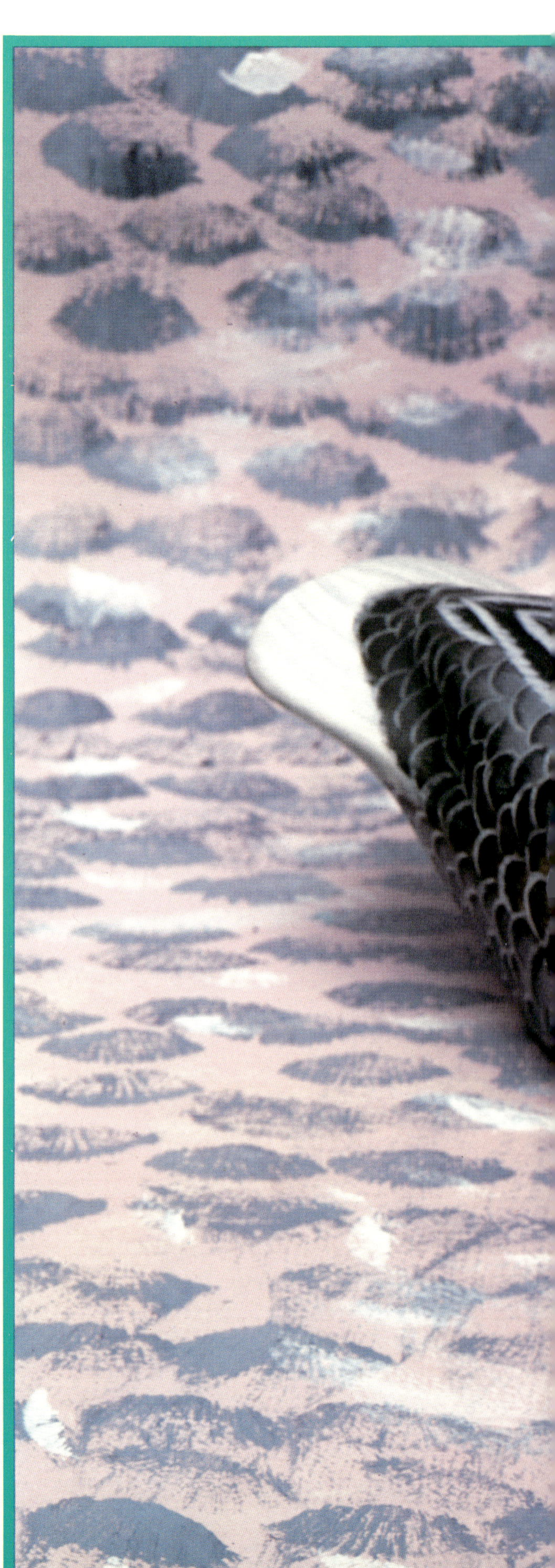

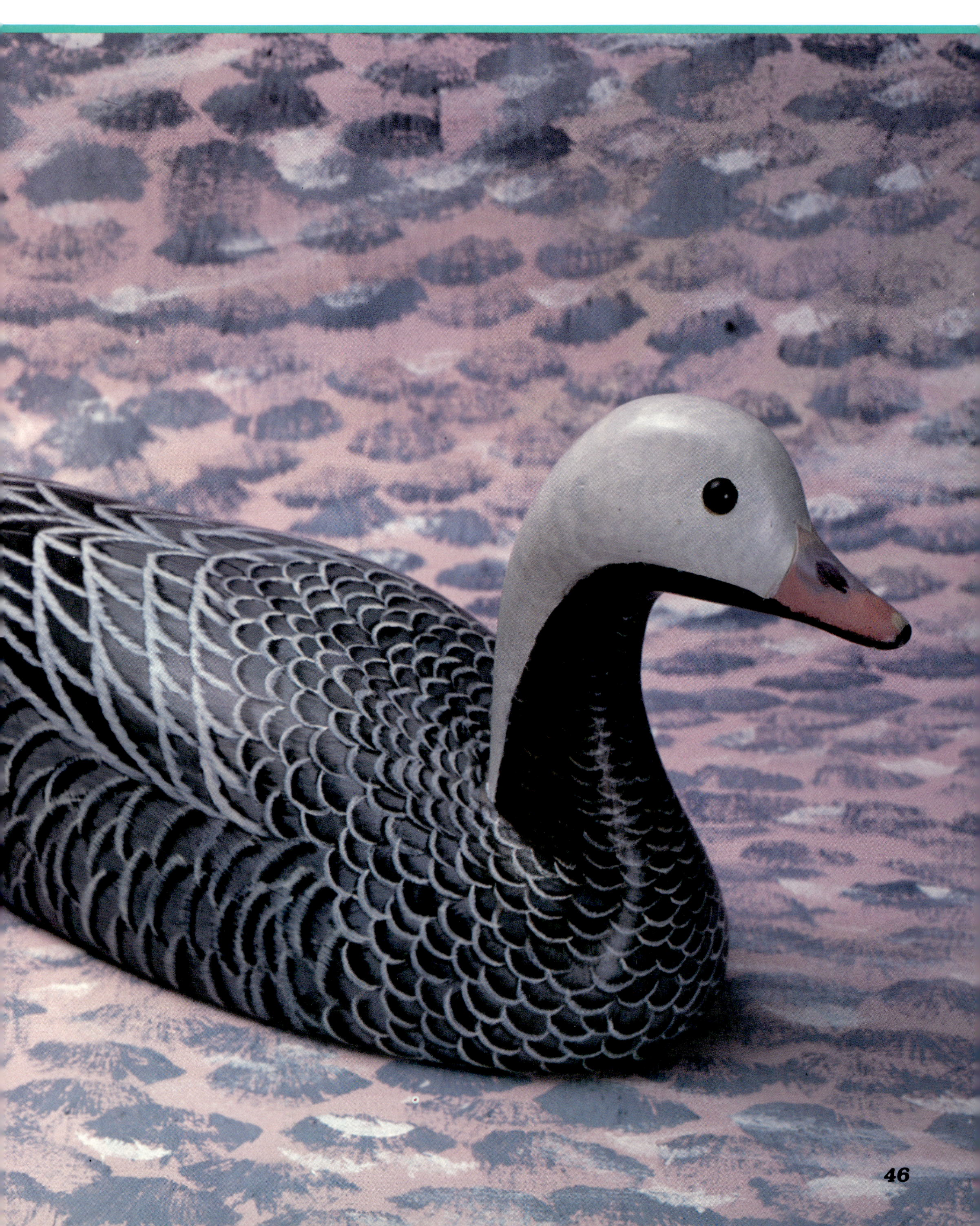

EMPEROR GOOSE

Permalba Colors

Ivory Black
Titanium White
Unbleached Titanium
Paynes Gray
Cadmium Red Medium
Cadmium Orange

Brushes

Beebe Hopper Liner #0
Beebe Hopper Shader #10
Beebe Hopper Kats Tongue #12
Langnickel Kats Tongue #18

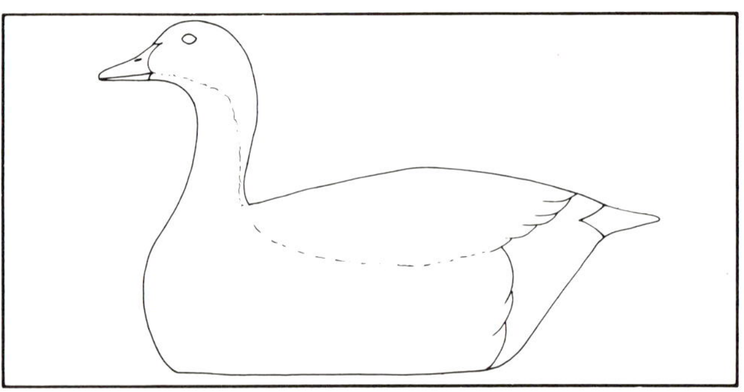

Illustration #39

Color placement diagram (Side view). Follow diagram to outline areas of color.

Titanium White + Paynes Gray + Unbleached Titanium = Color mixture.

Illustration #42

Shown above are the color chips for the mixture used to base the underneck, sides, back and rump of the Emperor Goose. Mix Titanium White and Paynes Gray with Unbleached Titanium to make a silver gray.

Draw in abstract areas to be painted using Illustration #39 as a guide.

TAIL

Paint tail area Titanium White mixed with a touch of Unbleached Titanium. Draw in feather pattern with pale gray using the Beebe Hopper Liner #0. Refer to Illustrations #40 and #41. Shade from outer edge inward with a white mixture of Unbleached Titanium and Titanium White using the Beebe Hopper Shader #10. If not distinctive enough, apply a second coat of white shading.

BODY: UNDERNECK, SIDES, BACK, AND RUMP

Apply coat of silver gray mixed from Titanium White, Gray and Unbleached Titanium. Refer to Illustration #42. Draw in feather

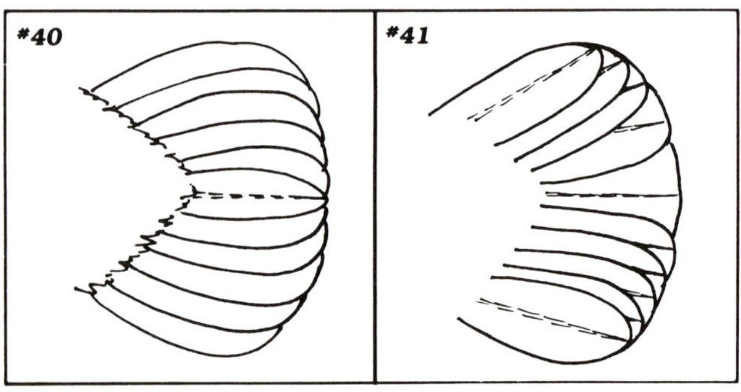

Illustration #40

Feather placement diagram (Top view). Follow diagram for general placement of featherstrokes for tail section.

Illustration #41

Feather placement diagram (Bottom view). Follow diagram for general placement of featherstrokes on tail sections.

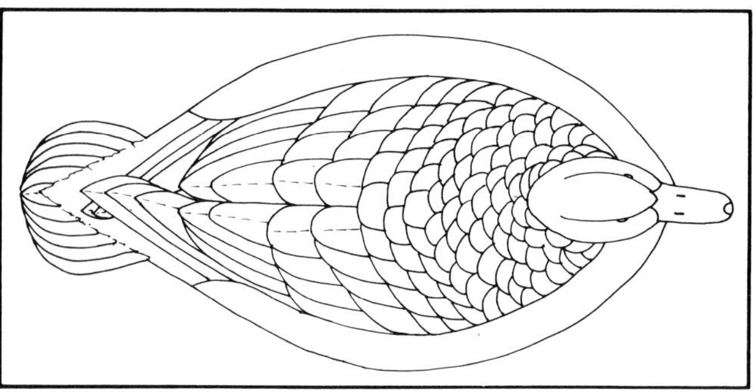

Illustration #43

Feather placement diagram (Top view). Follow diagram for general placement of featherstrokes on primary and tail sections.

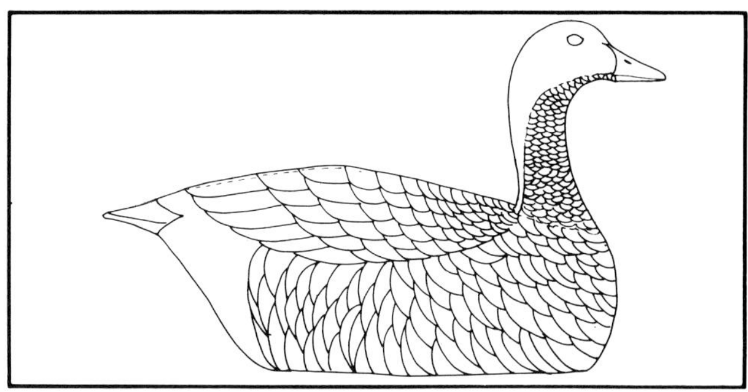

Illustration #44

Feather placement diagram (Side view). Follow diagram for general placement of featherstrokes on neck, wing and tail areas.

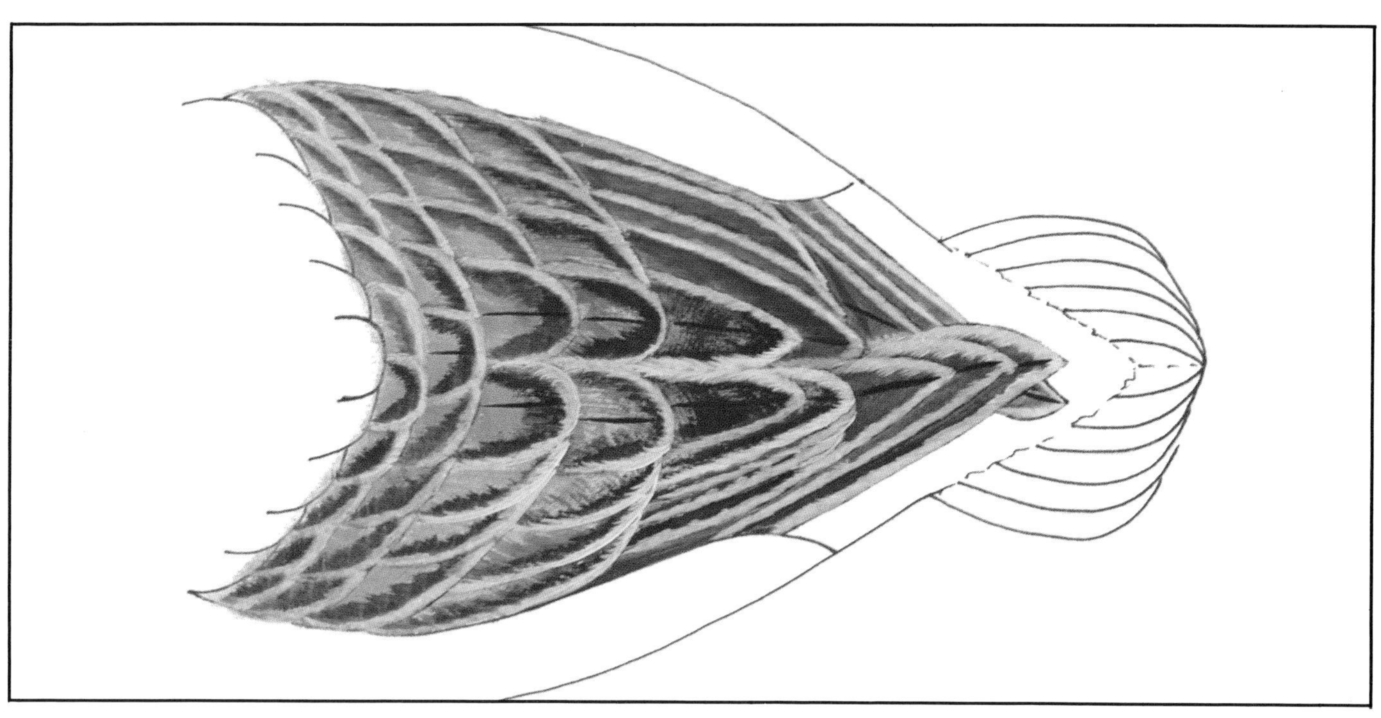

Illustration #45

Shade the tip of the feathers on the primaries with a mixture of Titanium White and Unbleached Titanium.

pattern of these areas using Beebe Hopper Liner #0. Refer to Illustrations # 43 and # 44 for feather layout. Shade in each individual feather with Black, being careful to leave silver color at the base of the feathers. Thin paint and soft strokes are a necessity. Less silver gray color is apparent on the underneck and chest. A narrow shading of White with a touch of Unbleached Titanium is then applied to the tip of the black feathers along the back, sides and lower chest. Refer to Illustration #45.

HEAD, BACK AND NECK

Apply coats of Titanium White mixed with a touch of Unbleached Titanium to lessen the chalky appearance.

BILL

Pink mottled with blue around nostrils. Lower mandible is flecked with black. Nail is off white.

EYE

Brown

EMPEROR GOOSE

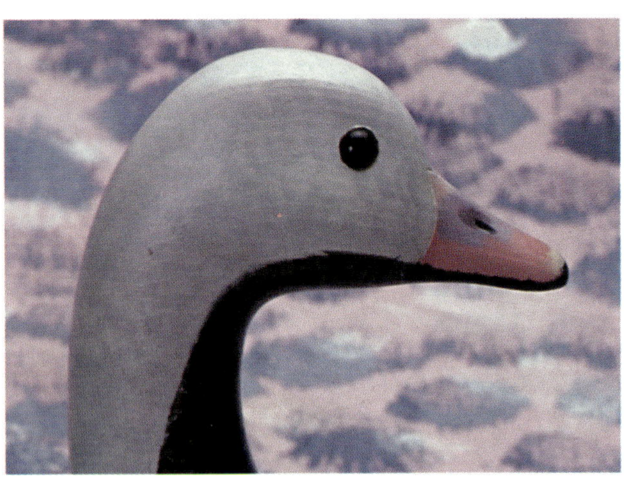

Detail - *Head Area*
The head area of the Emperor Goose is quite pale. Note the subtle featherstroke and the small amount of silver gray on the underneck.

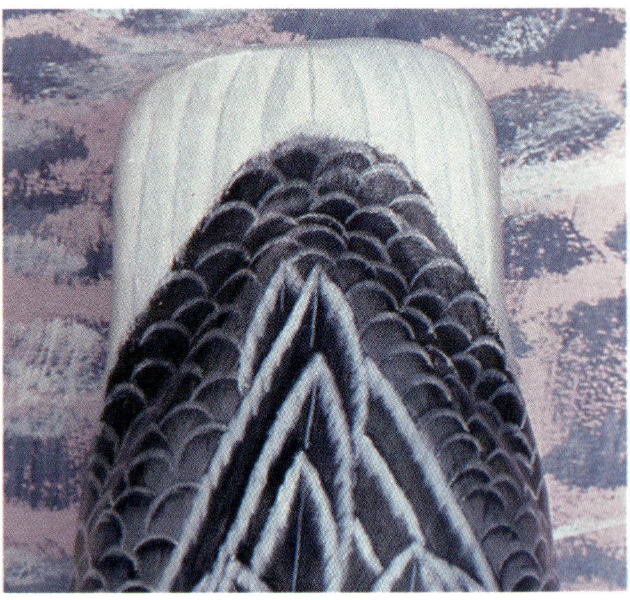

Detail - *Tail Area*
Take note of the stroke direction of the feathers in the tail area. The white highlights are quite distinctive.

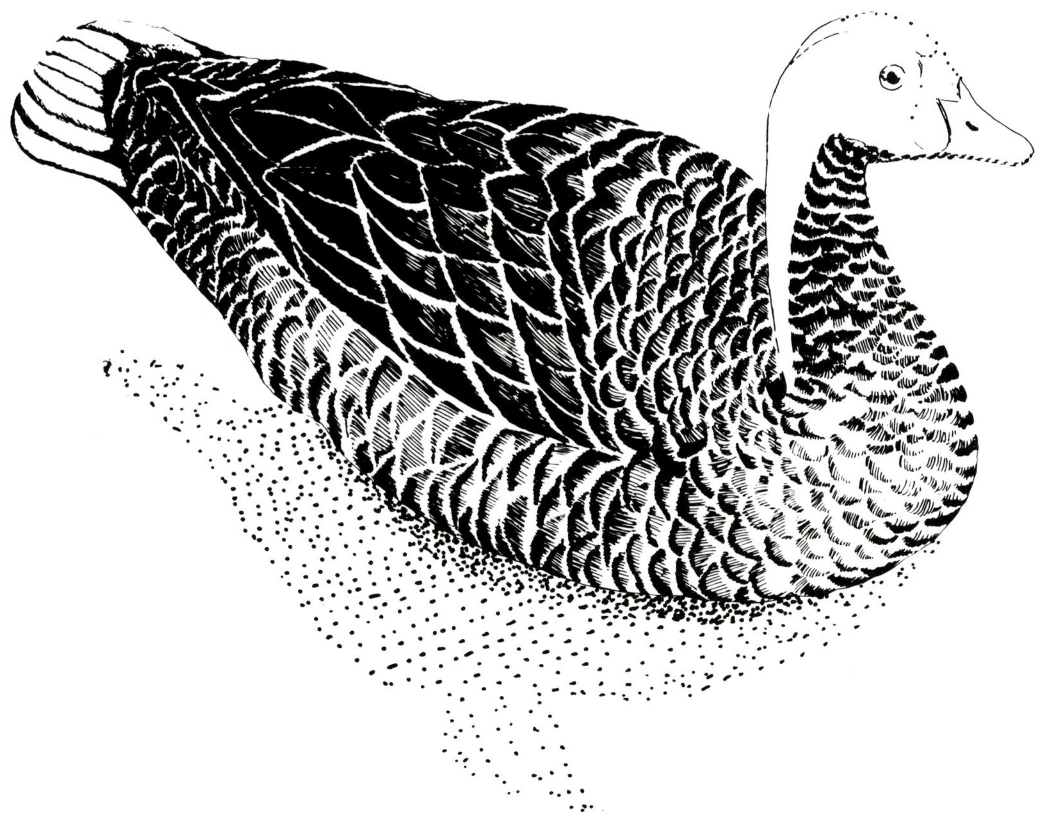

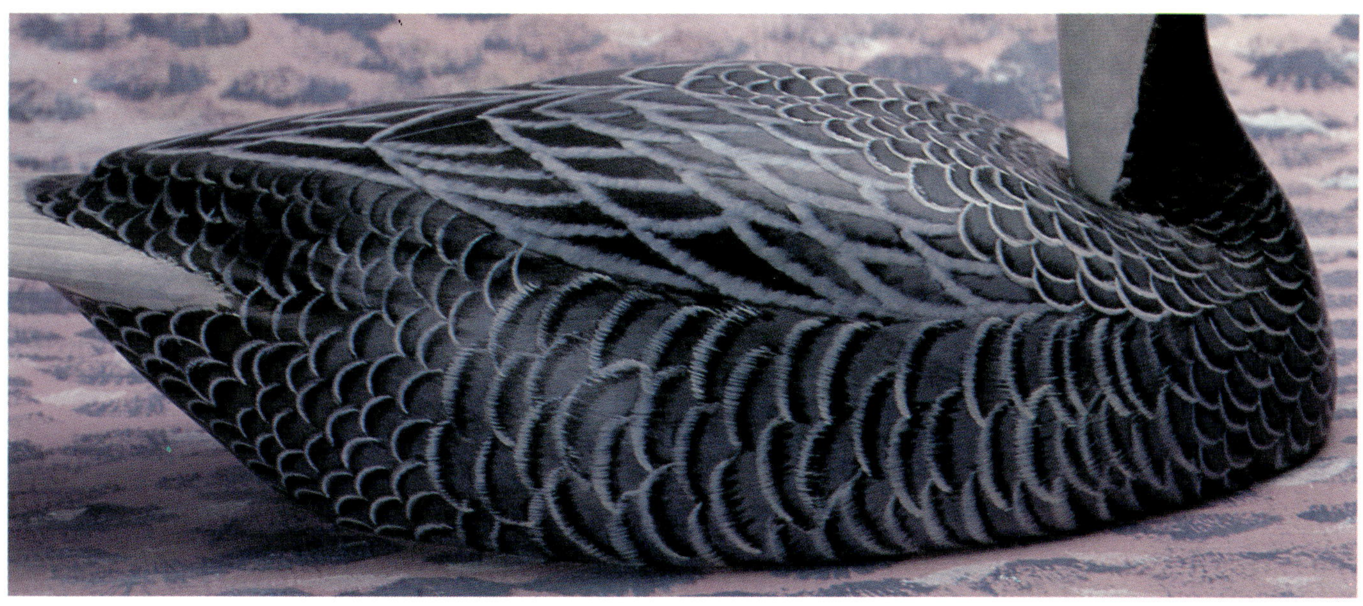

Detail - *Side Area*

    Refer to this close-up photograph for stroking on feathers on the side area of the Emperor Goose. Note the gradiation of size of the neck feathers to side feathers, to rump feathers.

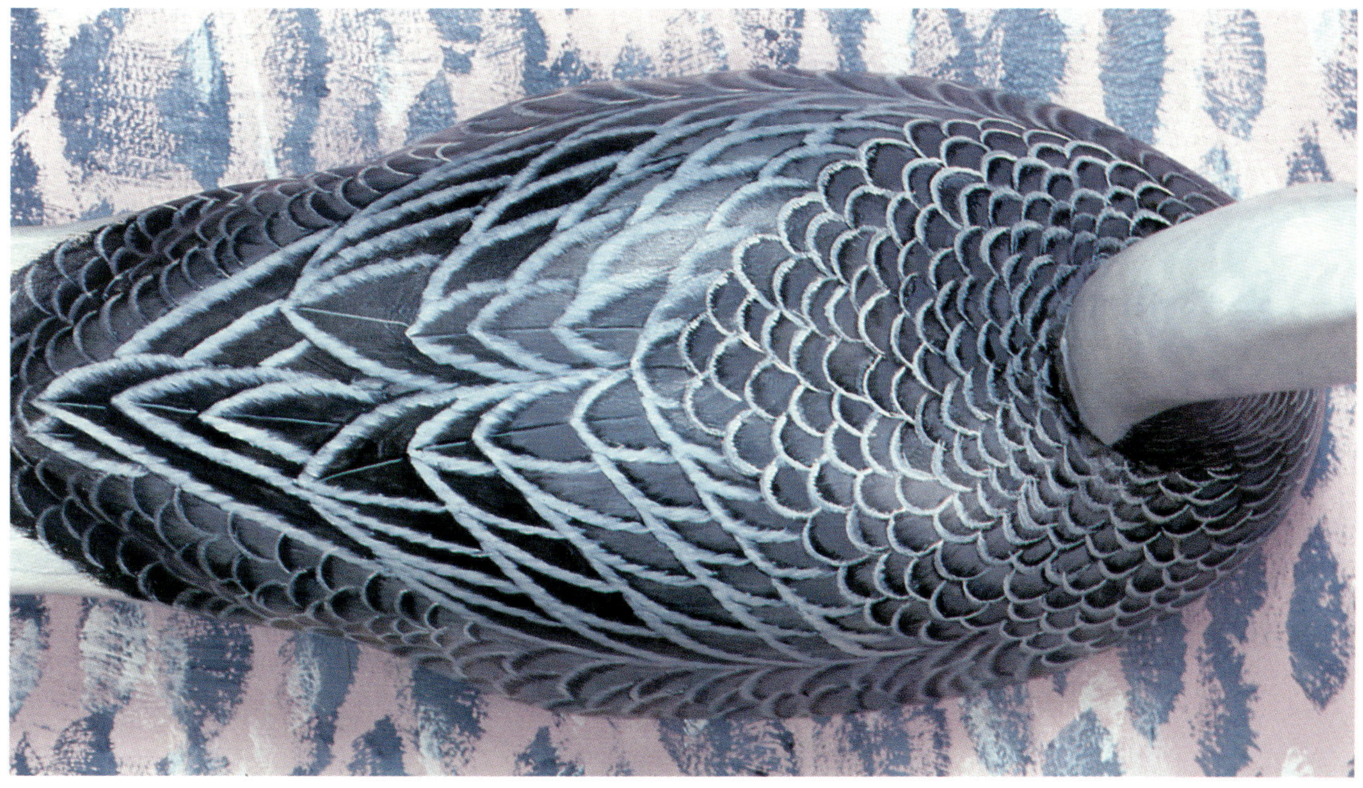

Detail - *Back Area*

    The feather pattern on the back area of the Emperor Goose is crisp and handsome.

BLACK BRANT

There are two species of Brant in North America, the Atlantic Brant and the Black Brant of the Pacific Coast. They are very similar except that the Black Brant is darker in color. Brant are small, sea-going geese that feed on eel grass and other marine vegetation in coastal areas of both coasts. They are handsome birds, their necks encircled with delicate white feather necklaces. They swim high and proud on the water unless they are disturbed at which time they swim low in the water with their necks stretched forward.

During winter months, flocks numbering several hundred birds can be found along tidal estuaries of the Atlantic and along the Pacific coast southward into Mexico. The flight of the Brant is very low over water, and for safety reasons, quite high over land. They do not necessarily follow a formation when flying, but are likely to form wide ranks.

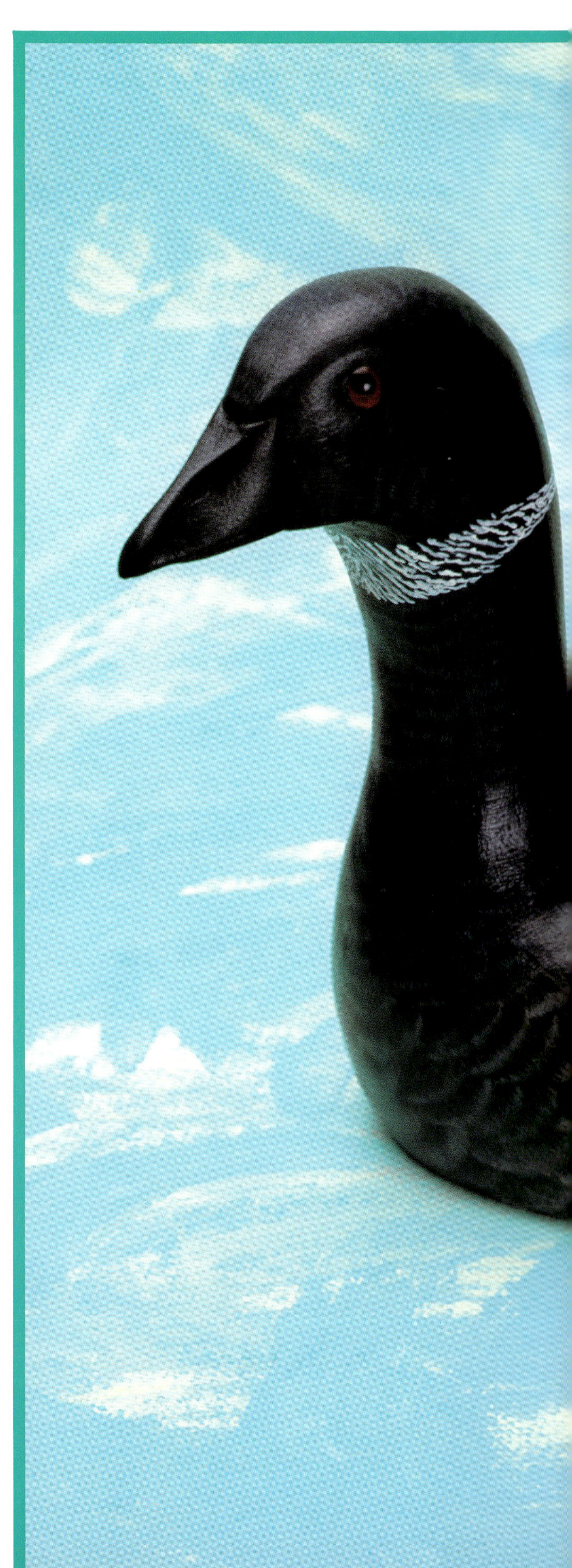

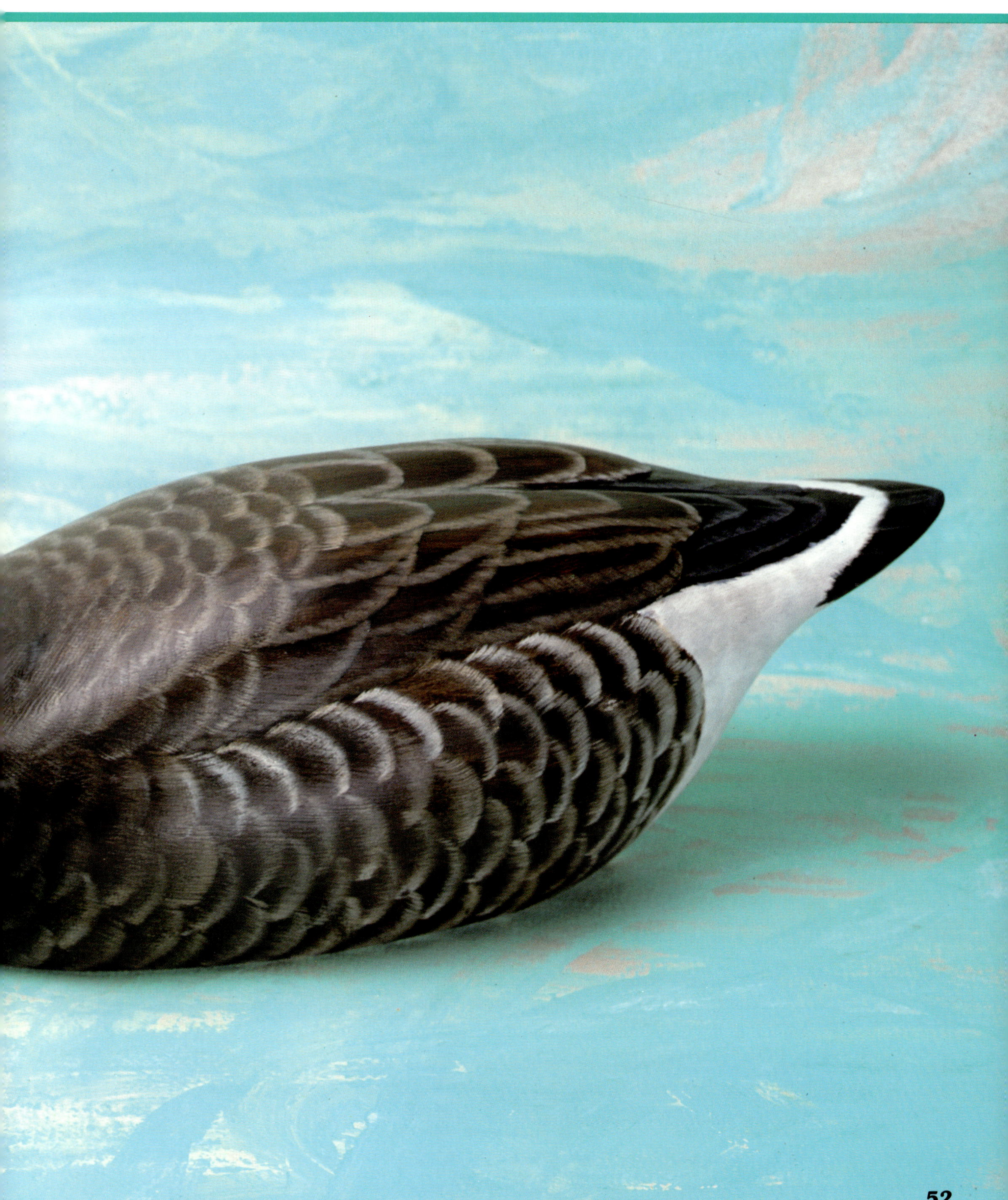

BLACK BRANT

Permalba Colors

Titanium White
Ivory Black
Unbleached Titanium
Raw Umber

Brushes

Beebe Hopper Liner #0
Beebe Hopper Shader #10
Beebe Hopper Kats Tongue #12
Langnickel Kats Tongue #18

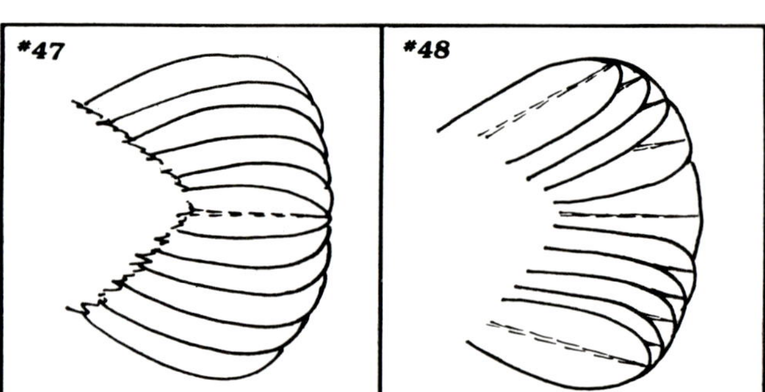

Illustration #46
Color placement diagram (Side view). Follow diagram to outline areas of color.

Prior to painting the Brant, you should sand the decoy to ensure that it is smooth. Apply a wood sealer to the whole decoy and let dry. When dry, apply a prime coat of paint. Lightly sand again when prime coat is dry.

Draw in abstract areas to be painted referring to Illustration #46 as a guide.

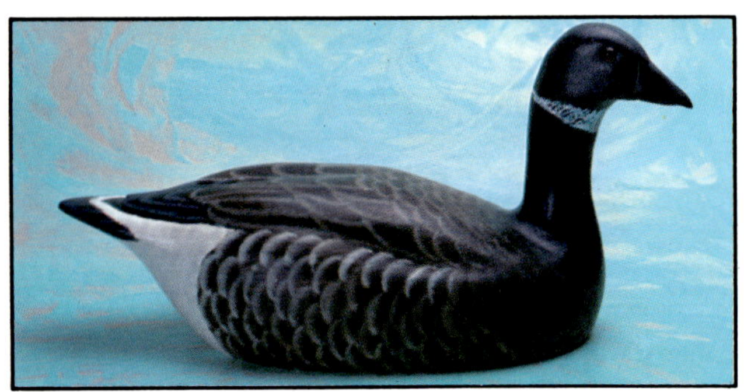

Illustration #47
Feather placement diagram (Top view). Follow diagram for general placement of featherstrokes for tail sections.

Illustration #48
Feather placement diagram (Bottom view). Follow diagram for general placement of featherstrokes for tail section.

TAIL

Paint tail area with Black. Using the Beebe Hopper Liner #0, draw in feather pattern referring to Illustrations #47 and #48 as a guide. With thin paint and soft strokes, shade from the outer edge inward with Titanium White and a touch of Unbleached Titanium using the Beebe Hopper Shader #10.

RUMP

Apply Titanium White with a touch of Unbleached Titanium to upper and lower rump. Ensure that paint is smooth and even. To create feather pattern, use Titanium White with a tiny amount of Black to make a *light* gray. Using the Beebe Hopper Kats Tongue

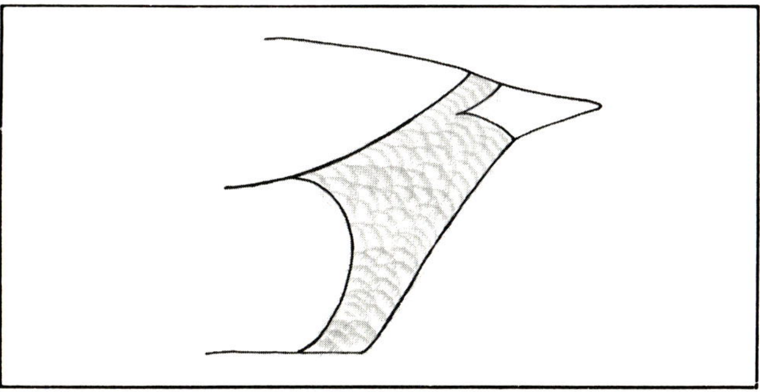

Illustration #49
Refer to the contour of feather placement for rump area of the Black Brant.

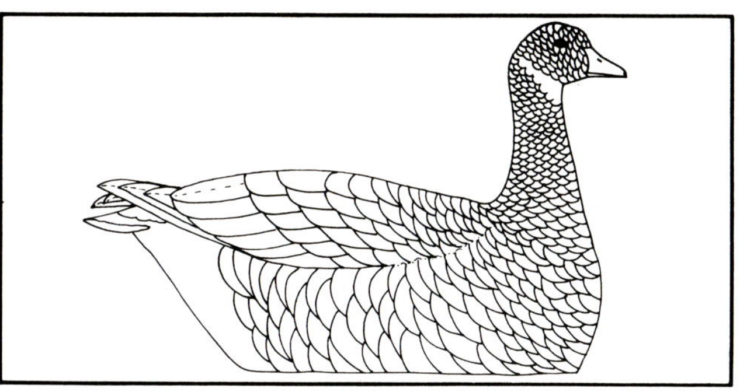

Illustation #50
Feather placement diagram (Side view). Follow diagram for general placement of featherstrokes on the head, neck, wing and tail areas.

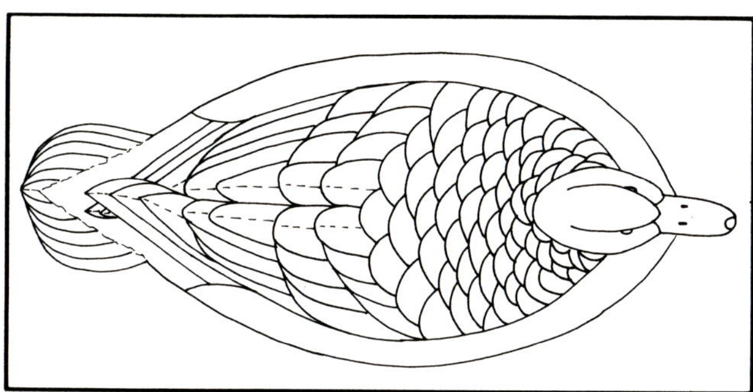

Illustration #51
Feather placement diagram (Top view). Follow diagram for general placement of featherstrokes on primary and wing sections.

#12, make feather pattern over area, following contour of feathers. Apply a wash of white mix if the feather pattern is too harsh. Refer to Illustration #49.

PRIMARIES AND SECONDARIES

Paint area with black. Draw in feather pattern for primaries and secondaries with dark gray

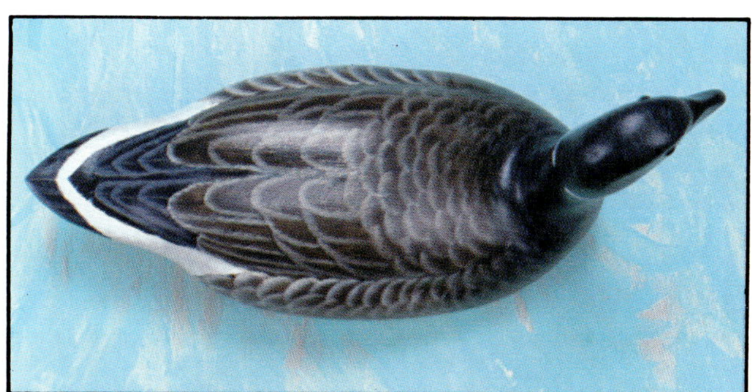

paint. Refer to Illustrations #50 and #51 for feather layout. Shade inward from outer edge with a mix of Black and Unbleached Titanium to make a dark gray using the Beebe Hopper Shader #10.

BACK, SHOULDERS AND SIDES

Apply Raw Umber to whole area. Draw in feather pattern with Black using Beebe Hopper Liner #0. Refer to Illustrations #50 and #51 for feather layout. Using the Langnickel Kats Tongue #18 and Unbleached Titanium with a touch of Titanium White, brush on feather pattern over whole area. Apply a wash of Raw Umber. Repeat procedure until desired soft - ness is achieved. The highlights on these fea - thers should be inconspicuous. The rear side feathers are much lighter. Shade in these fea - thers with the White-Unbleached Titanium mix.

HEAD, NECK AND CHEST

Coat this area with Black, blending lower edge to soften between chest and sides. Mix a touch of Unbleached Titanium with Black to make dark gray. Using the Beebe Hopper Kats Tongue #12, apply feather pattern over head, neck and chest following contour of feathers. Refer to Illustration #50 for feather layout. If effect is too harsh, apply a thin wash of Black.

NECK RING

Using the Beebe Hopper Liner #0 and Titanium White, make delicate small strokes. The neckband is wider under neck and comes to a point on the side of the neck.

BILL
Black

EYE
Brown

BLACK BRANT

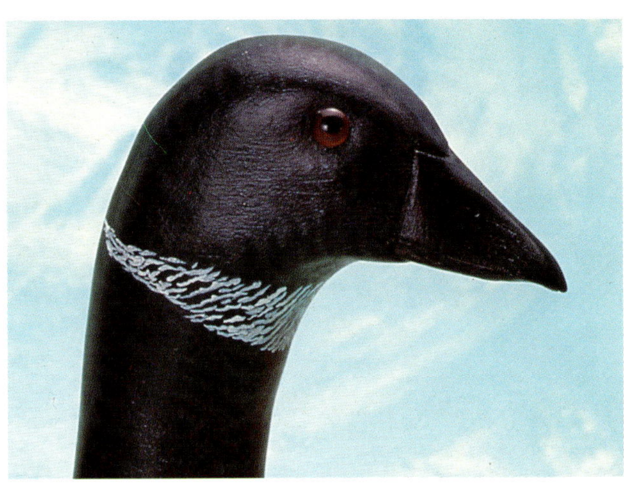

Detail - *Head Area*
    The head area of the Black Brant is painted in a dark tone with subtle feather pattern stroked on.

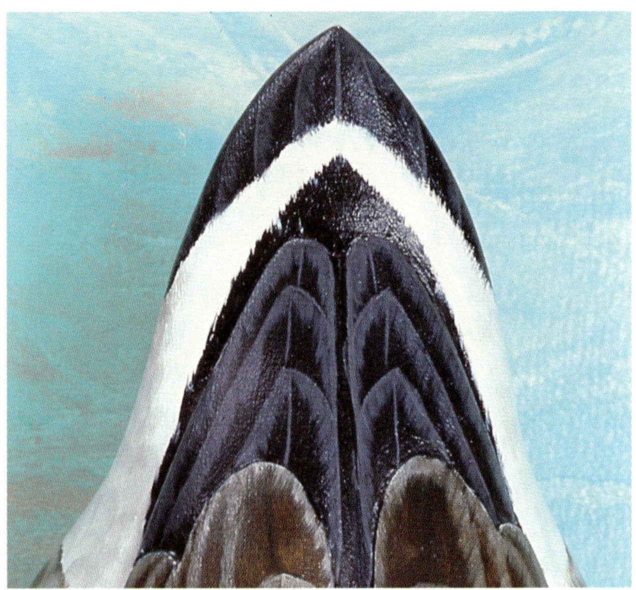

Detail - *Tail Area*
    Pay close attention to the direction of the feathers in the tail area.

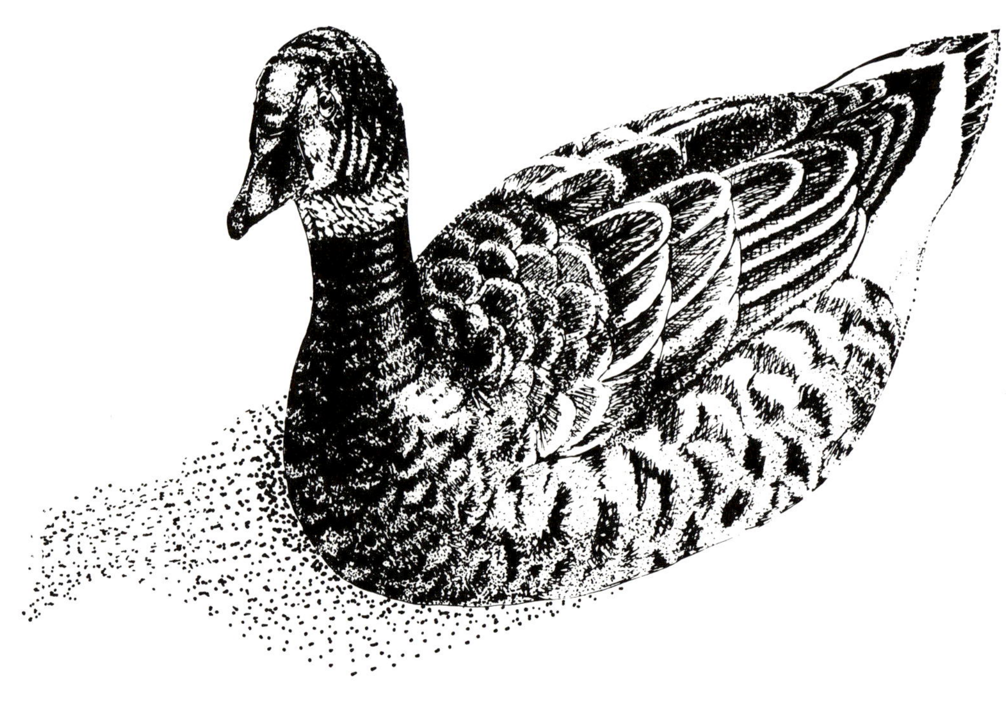

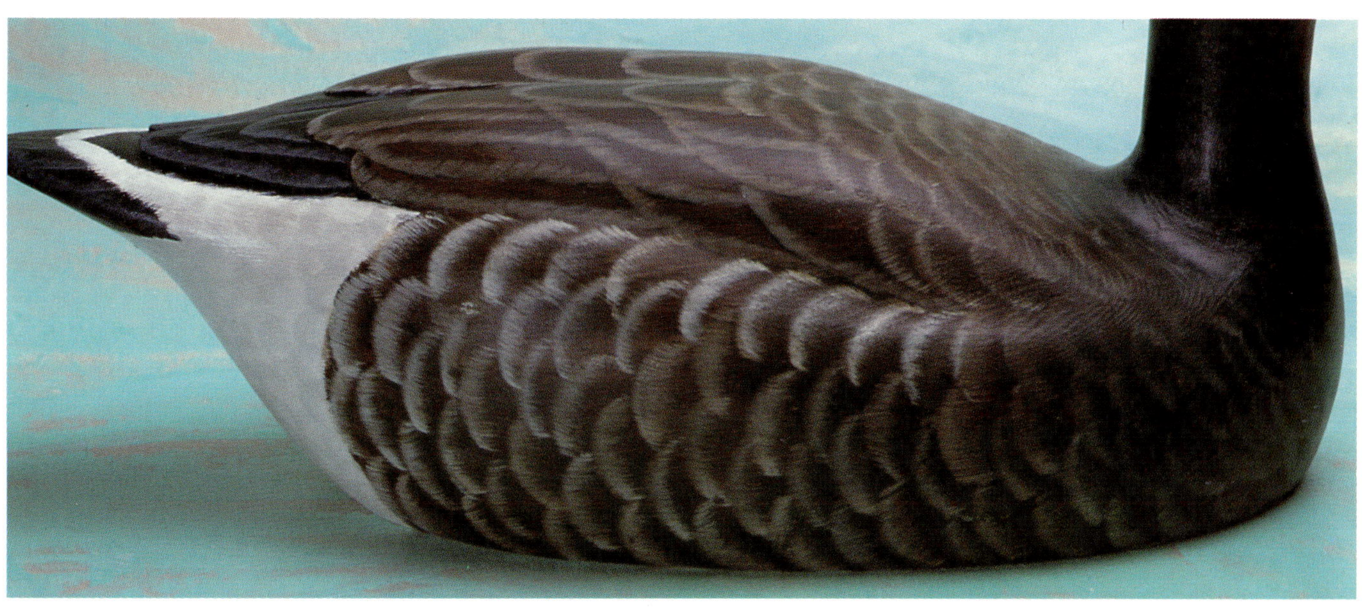

Detail - *Side Area*
   Refer to this close-up photograph for stroking on feathers and applying paint to the desired softness in the Black Brant. Note that the rear side feathers are much lighter.

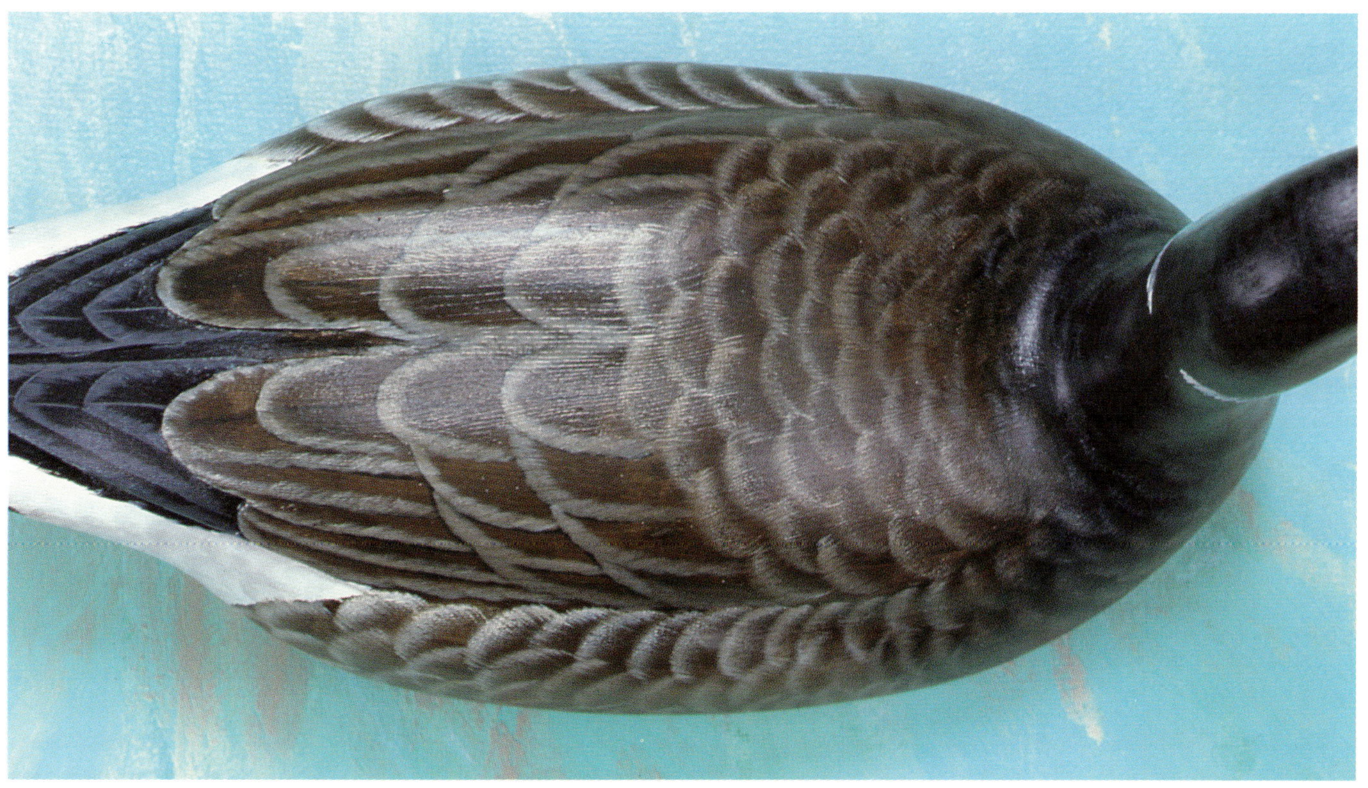

Detail - *Back Area*
   Feather pattern on the back area of the Black Brant.

PRAIRIE CANADAS

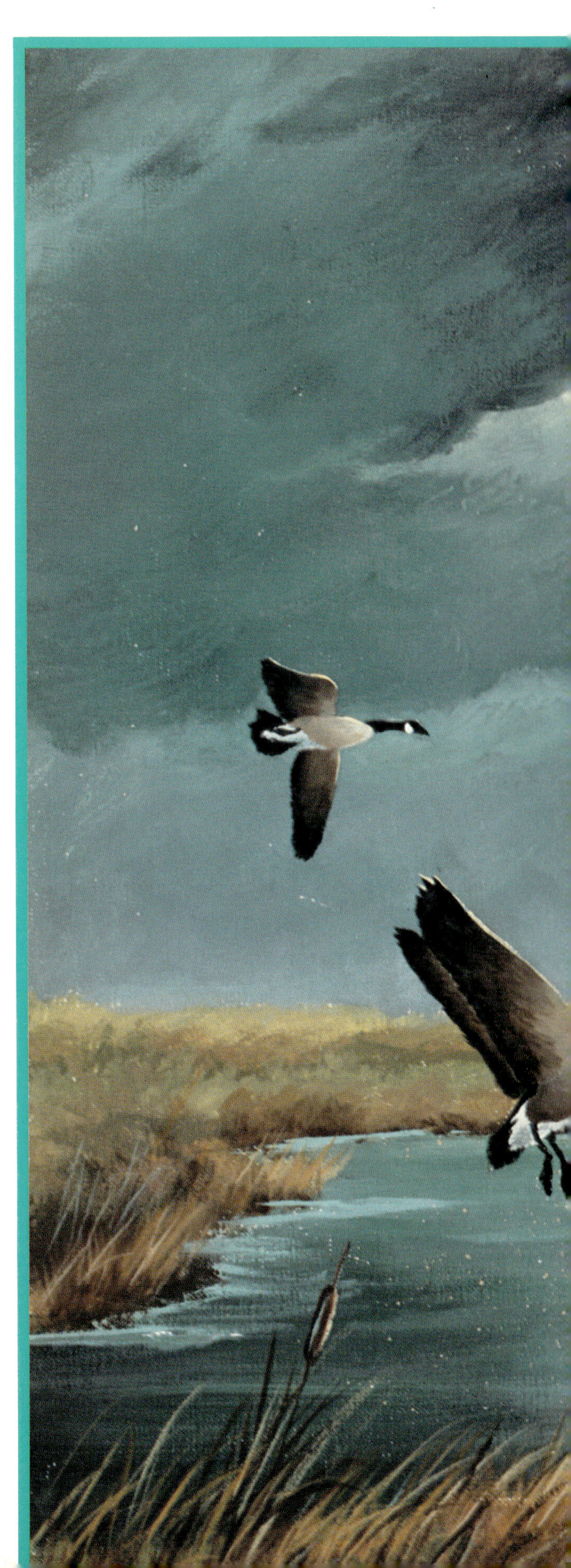

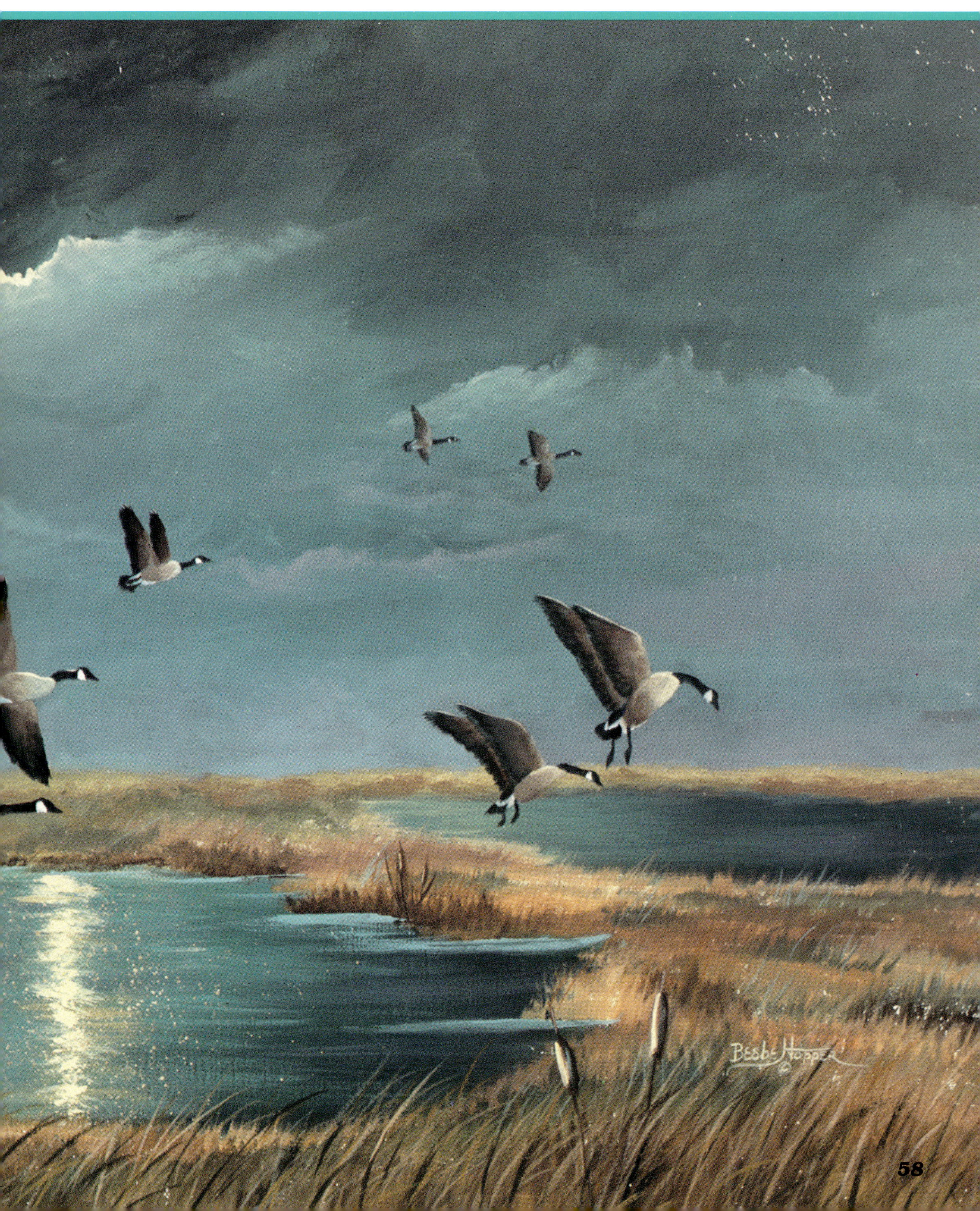
Besbe Hopper

PRAIRIE CANADAS

Permalba Colors

Titanium White
Unbleached Titanium
Phthalo Green
Alizarin Crimson
Raw Sienna
Burnt Sienna
Burnt Umber
Raw Umber
Ivory Black

Brushes

Beebe Hopper Liner #0
Beebe Hopper Shader #44
Beebe Hopper Kats Tongue #12

Phthalo Green + Alizarin Crimson = Color mixture

Illustration #52
   Shown here are color chips to create the mixture for the "parent" color used throughout the painting. Equal amounts of Phthalo Green and Alizarin Crimson are mixed together.

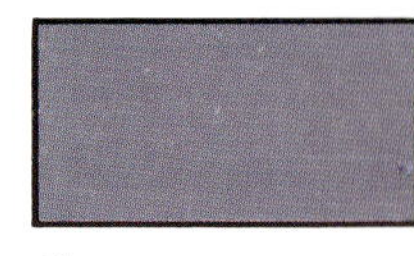

A   *B*   *C*

A. Titanium White + Parent color + Phthalo Green
B. Titanium White + Parent color
C. Titanium White + Parent color + Alizarin Crimson

Illustration #53
   Shown here are color chips to create the mixture for the sky and water areas.

When painting on canvas, I use the finest portrait linen canvas - Fredrix Kent 125 DP. The smooth surface of this canvas helps to conserve your brushes,whereas a coarse weave canvas wears brushes at a much faster rate. The brushes that I prefer to use are soft hair brushes. This gives soft, blended tones, which is the effect that I am trying to acheive.

Sketch the basic design on the canvas with a soft lead pencil or charcoal. Paint in the entire background: sky, water and marshlands first. When the painting is completely dry, super-impose the geese onto the background. Transfer the geese images using tracing paper with graphite paper. Beware of using carbon paper because it often leaves smudges. Graphite paper is the cleanest and easiest method of application.

This painting is completed with acrylics using a very limited palette for the sky colors. The marsh grass adds three earth tones and the geese an additional earth tone. Please keep in mind to always work wih a dampened canvas. Moisten the canvas with a clean sponge and water. This will enable you to blend the acrylic colors with very little effort and slow the fast drying qualities of acrylic paints.

Waterfowl habitat differs somewhat from area to area, however, "a marsh is a marsh" and the basics of painting a marsh remain constant. Salt water marshes differ from fresh water marshes in the surrounding flora and fauna. Acquaint yourself with the foliage common to the area that you wish to paint.

The "parent" color mixed for this painting is a very vibrant black made from equal amounts of Alizarin Crimson and Phthalo Green and mixed thoroughly. Refer to Illustration #52. With the addition of Titanium White to this mixture, you can produce a lovely sky blue. For cooler tones, add more Phthalo Green and for warmer tones, add more Alizarin Crimson. Refer to Illustration #53.

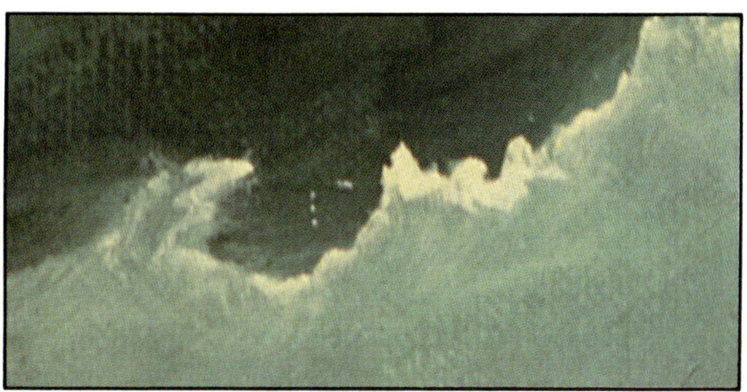

Illustration #54

Unbleached Titanium is used to paint in the sunlight in the sky. Start with the color full strength to accent the cloud edge, then gradually bend out into darker areas.

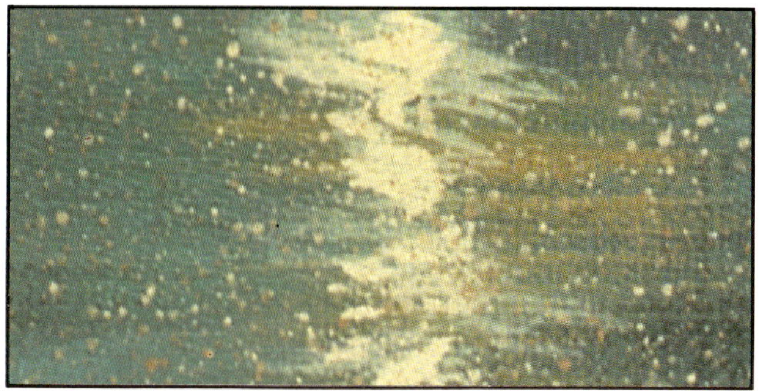

Illustration #55

The sparkles on the water are Unbleached Titanium. Thin paint consistency and flick color onto the canvas with a tooth brush.

Sky and Clouds

Using the Beebe Hopper Kats Tongue #12 or the Beebe Hopper Shader #44, paint the sky with the "parent" color mixed with Unbleached Titanium and/or Titanium White to create variations of tonal clouds and sky areas. The sunlight area is painted with Unbleached Titanium. Use the color full strength along the cloud edge, gradually working the color into the darker areas of the sky. Refer to Illustration #54. Add a touch of Alizarin Crimson to the lighter sky mixture to give the appearance of distance along the horizon. The entire sky is painted using only four colors: Phthalo Green, Alizarin Crimson, Unbleached Titanium and Titanium White.

Water

The same colors are used in the water that are used in the sky. This is because water acts like a mirror, reflecting all the colors and shapes surrounding it. The sun's reflection is

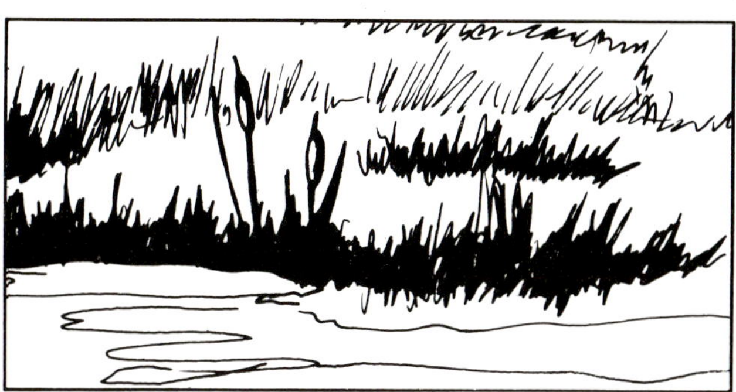

painted with Unbleached Titanium. The sparkles on the water are applied by flicking thinned Unbleached Titanium onto the canvas with a tooth brush. Refer to Illustration #55 for the finished effect of this technique.

Grass

Using the Beebe Hopper Shader #44 with an upward flicking motion, paint in the marsh grass areas. The grasses on the horizon are painted with a mix of Raw Sienna and Unbleached Titanium muted with a tiny amount of the sky color mixture. For the other grasses, add Burnt Sienna and Burnt Umber to your palette. Place the colors randomly throughout the grass areas in the painting. Remember to paint all the grasses using an upward flicking motion. The taller grass detail in the foregound is painted with the grass mix, Burnt Sienna and Raw Sienna using the Beebe Hopper Liner #0. Cattails are added using Raw Umber with Unbleached Titanium highlights and the sky mixture for shading.

Canada Geese

The colors used for the Canada Geese are Raw Umber, Black, Titanium White, and Unbleached Titanium. The wings are shaded from a lightened Raw Umber to a dark black-brown color. Stroke on colors to give the appearance of feathers. The head, feet and tail are painted black. Under rump and cheek patch are Titanium White with a touch of the sky mixture for shading. The bodies of the geese are based in Raw Umber highlighted with Unbleached Titanium at the chest.

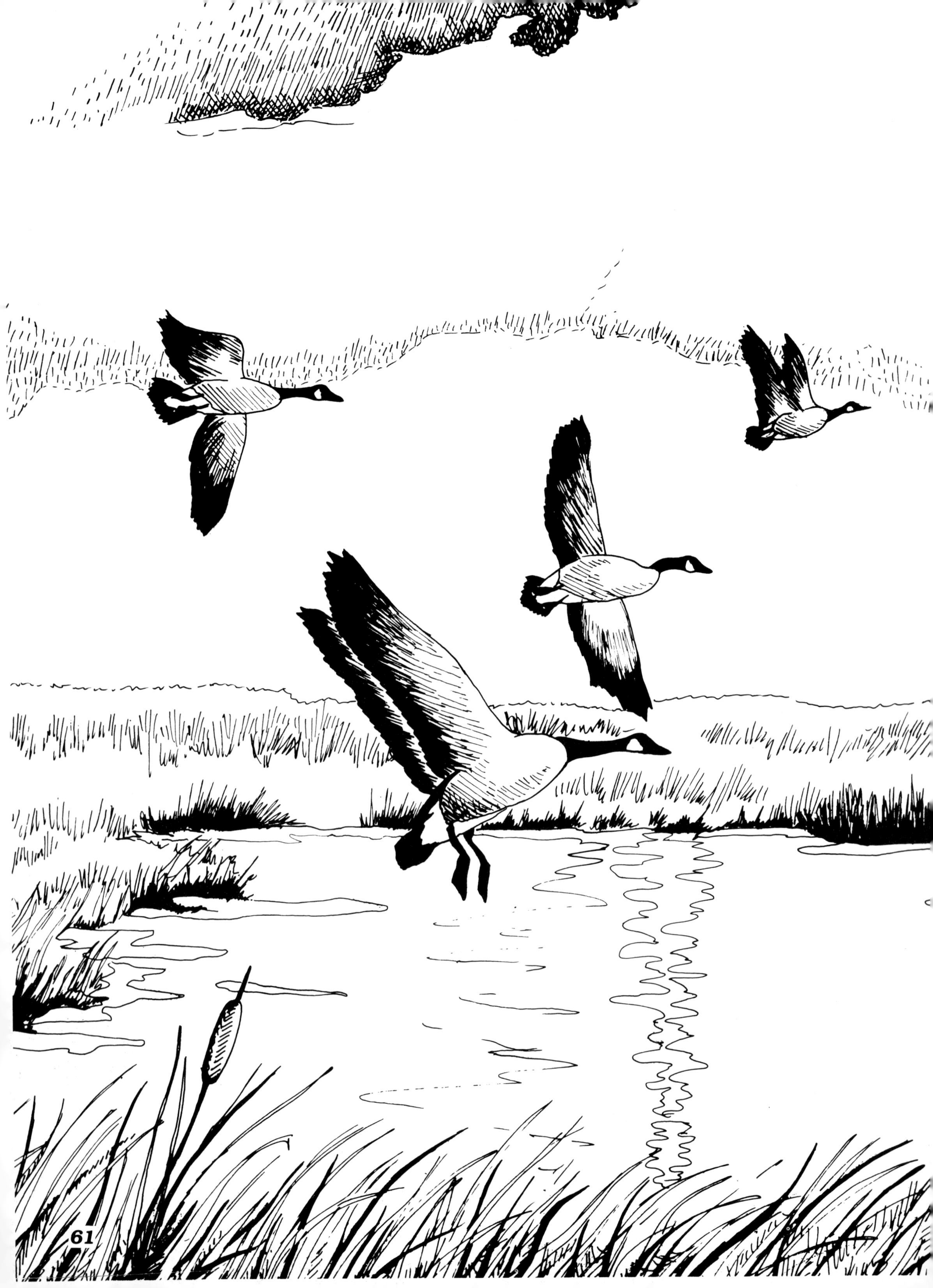

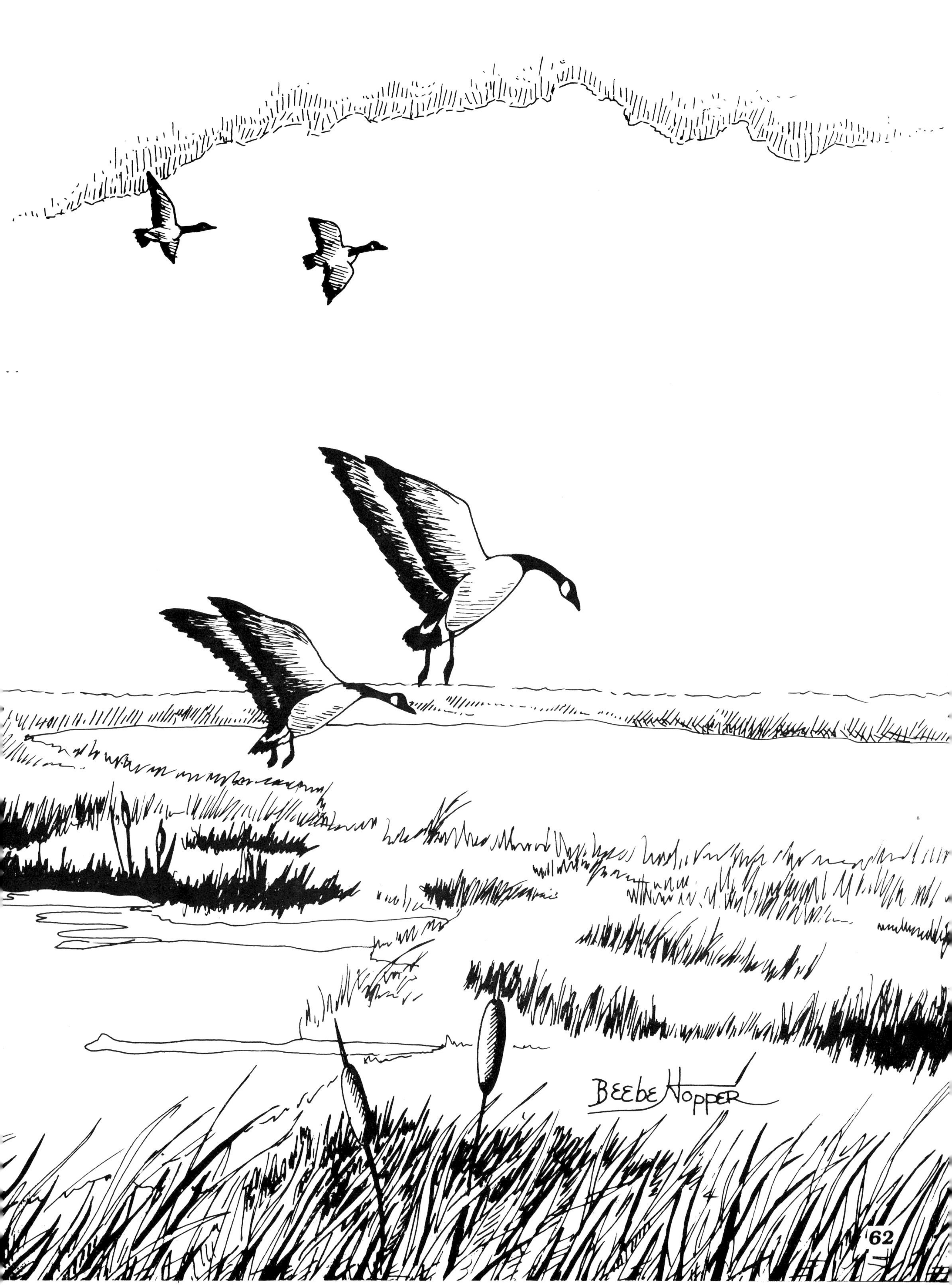
Beebe Hopper

HISTORY OF DECOY CARVING

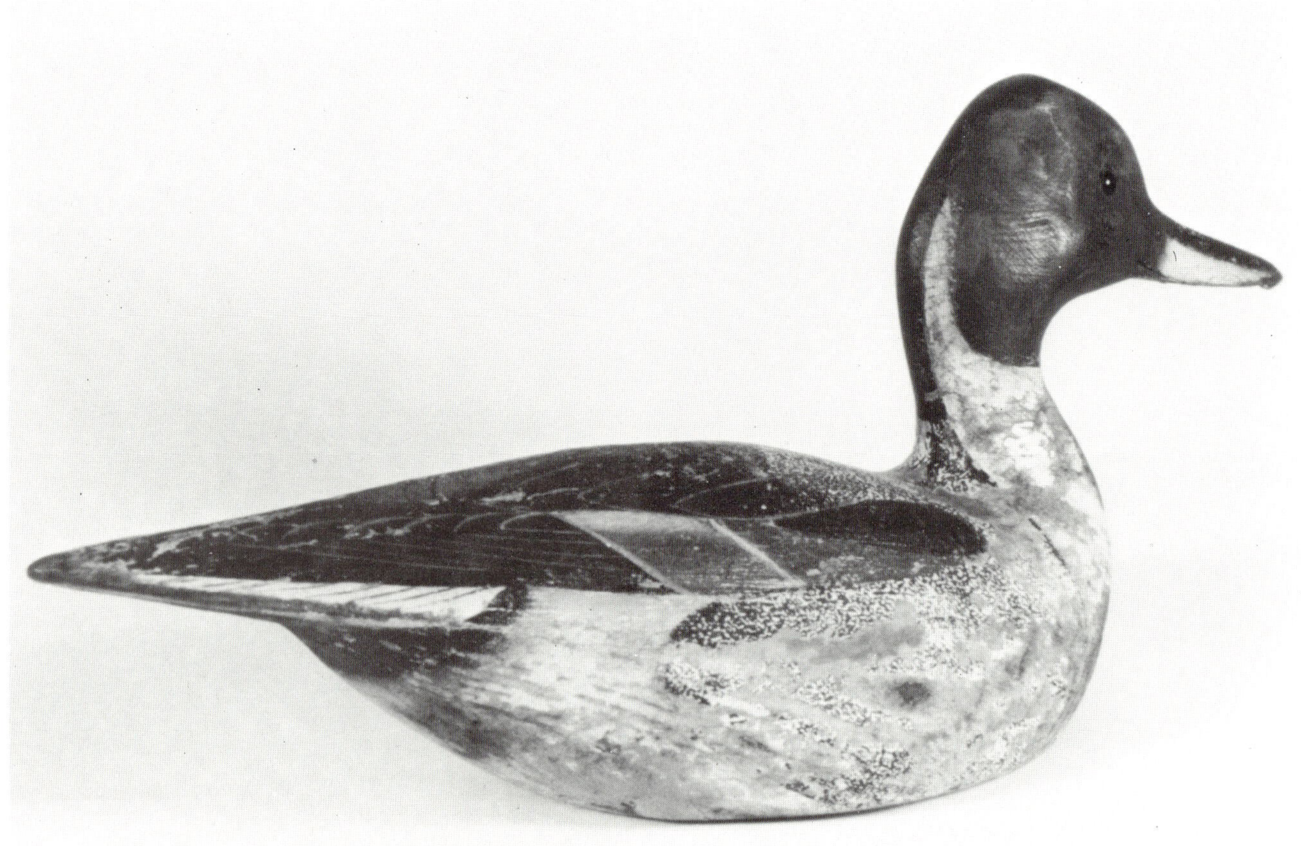

Ward Pintail - **1936,** *Ward Foundation Collection*

History of Decoy Carving

Of the many types of American Folk Art - weathervanes, cigar store indians, barbershop poles - perhaps the most original is the decoy. Defined by World Book Dictionary as "an artificial bird used to lure birds into a trap or within gunshot", the decoy has maintained its allure for sportsmen, collectors and artisans for centuries.

In 1924, an archaeological find in Lovelock Cave, Nevada revealed a beautifully preserved group of decoys dating back more than a thousand years. Several of them, cleverly depicting the canvasback duck, were made of woven tule grass colored with the dyes that the American Indians made from natural substances. Indians used white feathers along the sides of the decoy to provide a realistic look to the form. The whole body was then bound with a fine cord or line. These ancient decoys are on display at the North American Indian Museum in New York City and were the beginning of the art form as we know it today.

Early settlers in America depended upon wild game for food and found many uses for the feathers of wildfowl. They took their cue from the Indians and fashioned decoys to draw waterfowl into close range of both gun and arrow.

The growing population in America lead to the inception of market hunting. This new breed of hunter killed and sold wild game birds to the general population. They utilized large numbers of decoys in their "rigs", enabling them to mass kill anything on the wing to fill orders for the growing market. No bird was exempt - songbirds, waterfowl and shorebirds were all included.

Because of the increasing number of decoys demanded for market hunters' rigs, and the amount of time required to carve a decoy, the hand carvers were no longer able to keep up with production.

American ingenuity soon produced the first factory made decoys and a new business was born. Decoys were manufactured by the thousands to provide for the "market hunters" as well as for the sportsman. Today, these machine made birds are highly valued as collector's items. Decoys manufactured by Mason, Evans, Pratt, Stevens and others bring tremendous prices at decoy auctions.

In 1918, the Congress of the United States passed the Migratory Bird Treaty Act, which outlawed the killing of migratory birds. With the passage of the act, the demand for factory-made decoys declined rapidly. In recent years, however, the machine made birds have made a comeback and the business of manufacturing

of the machine made bird, hand made decoys continued to be crafted for carvers own collections and a small commercial demand. Many of these old time carvers are now considered to be the "Old Masters" of American Folk Art and their works are prized and sought after by collectors. Elmer Crowell, Nathan Cobb, Joe Lincoln, Charles Wheeler, Charles Perdew, Bill Bowman, Harry Shourds, and Steve and Lem Ward are a few of the most notable carvers from this era.

The Chesapeake Bay and surrounding areas were and still are considered one of the prime waterfowl areas for hunters and bird watchers alike. In the early 1900's on the eastern shore town of Crisfield, Maryland, Steve and Lem Ward were barbers who spent their off time carving decoys. Generally, Steve did the carving and Lem did the painting. Through the years,

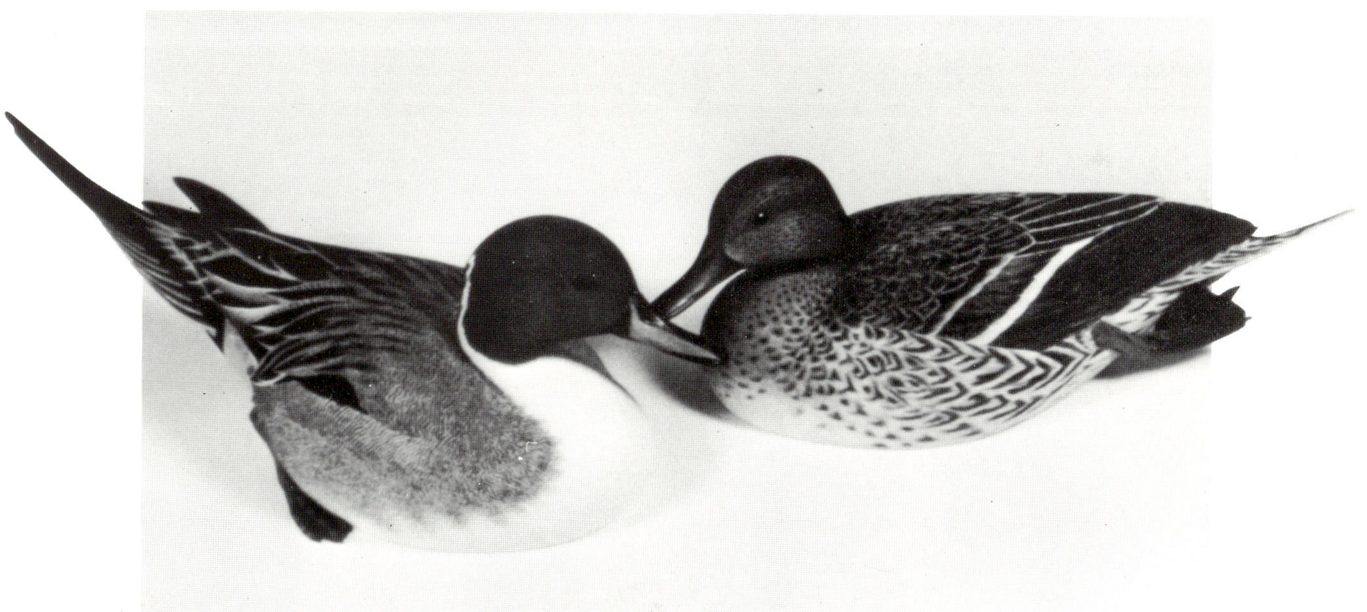

Pintails: Hen and Drake - *Tan Brunet,* **Best in World Decorative Decoy Pair - 1977**

decoys is thriving again. In addition to birds used by sportsmen for their shooting rigs, there is a new market for artists, craftsmen, and tole and decorative painters. Carvers and artists enhance the basic decoy by painting, woodburning feather patterns, and inserting feathers to make the wooden blanks look more realistic.

During both the rise to and fall from popularity

they pioneered the evolution from functional decoys to the more current decorative poses. They inserted feathers and gave their birds legs to better express and add realism to their craft. The Ward brothers carved for over fifty years and produced approximately 25,000 decoys. After the death of Steve in 1976, Lem continued painting, drawing and writing poetry until his death in 1984. The collection of a serious decoy enthusiast would not be complete without a Ward Brothers decoy.

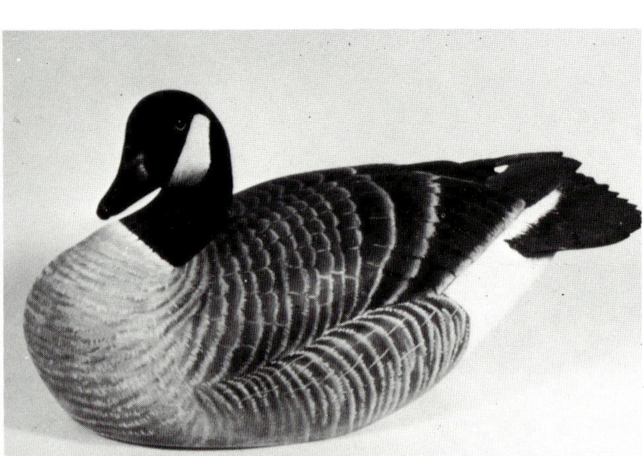

Canadian Goose - *Ward Brothers*

The Ward Foundation

The Ward Foundation, named for Steve and Lem Ward, was established in 1958 to promote and perpetuate interest in wildlife art, wildlife carving and conservation of both wildlife and natural resources. As an outgrowth of the Ward Foundation, the North American Wildlife Art Museum was established at Salisbury State College in Salisbury, Maryland in 1975. Over 3000 carvings and artifacts are on display at the museum, which follow the progress of decoy carving from the beginning of the artform to the present.

The Ward Foundation began the World Championship Carving Competition in 1971. The Competition moved from Salisbury, Maryland in 1978 and is held the last weekend of April each year at Convention Hall in Ocean City, Maryland. Approximately 2500 different carvings are entered in competition each year, representing the work of about 800 to 900 carvers from across the United States and Canada. The World Championship Carving Competition is considered to be one of the most prestigeous shows for carvers and the competition is intense.

The Waterfowl Festival

Easton, Maryland, home of The Waterfowl Festival, is a charming town of only 8000 residents with quaint shops, colonial architecture and the warmth common to the people of the eastern shore. In 1971, through the efforts of two Easton residents, Dr. Harry M. Walsh and Bill Perry, The Waterfowl Festival was born. Through the foresight and determination of these two men, the Waterfowl Festival has developed into the largest and most prestigeous show of its kind in the nation.

Today, more than 700 dedicated volunteers share in the preparation and staging of this tribute to wildfowl. Profits from this enormous effort are contributed to various wildlife organizations for the conservation and preservation of our natural resources and wildlife habitat.

On the second weekend of November each year, the very top names in waterfowl art - carvers, painters, sculptors, photographers and collectors are invited to participate in this show. During the event, Easton hosts more than 20,000 visitors, who tour the different exhibit

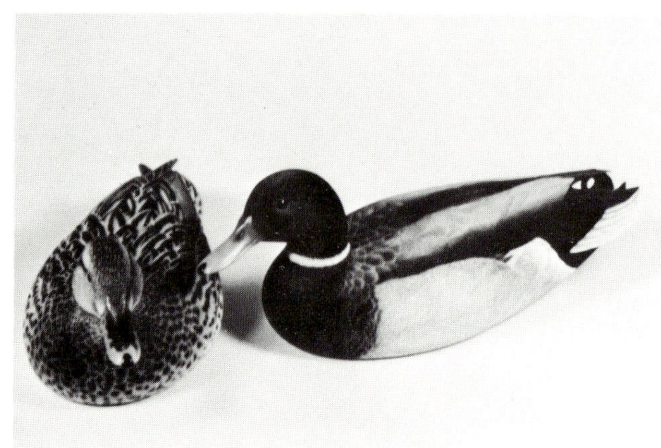

Decoy Competition - *1974*

areas via free shuttle buses on foot, directed by flying geese graphics that volunteers have painted on the sidewalks.

The Tidewater Inn serves as headquarters for

The Waterfowl Festival and houses the Gold Room, where the finest waterfowl art is displayed. The carvings displayed in the Armory are so lifelike, they seem as if they may take flight at any moment. Wildfowl photography is exhibited at the Academy of Arts and the firehouse is home for the workshop, where carvers and artists demonstrate their crafts.

Other attractions include gift shops, book corners, artifact exhibits, buy, sell and swap areas, a duck and goose calling contest and an auction of antique decoys. The collector, artist, nature enthusiast or home shopper is sure to find excitement and perhaps a few treasures at The Waterfowl Festival.

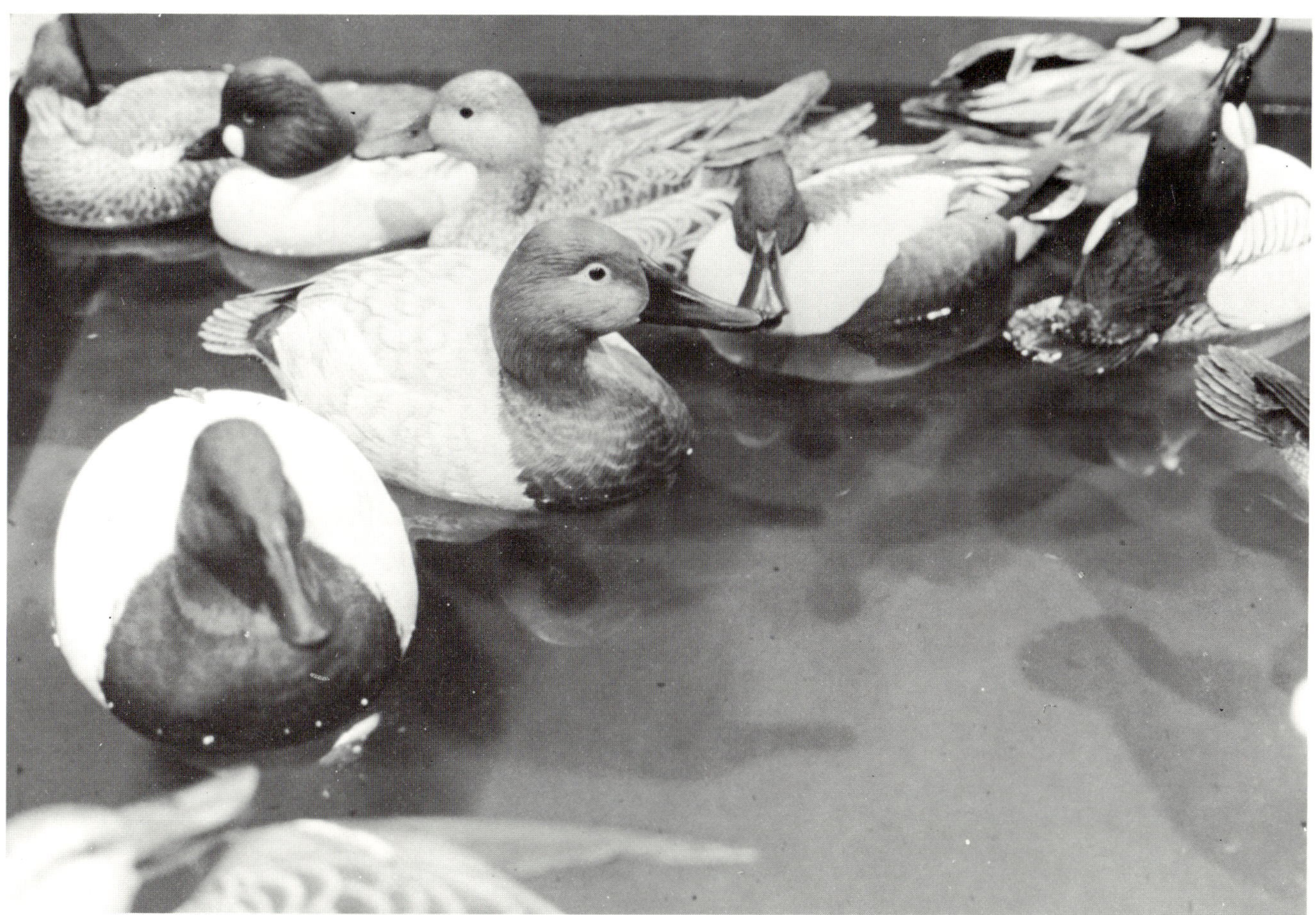

Decoy Competition - *1976, Ward Foundation*

Exhibits, Shows and Competitions

There are many bird carving and wildfowl art shows, both exhibition and competition, all across the nation. One of the remarks heard at many competitive shows today is "Don't put a live bird in the tank, he might take second place." This statement attests to the breathtaking realism found in a great many wildfowl carvings and paintings.

The first shows began about 35 years ago along the east coast. Today, many of them are still concentrated in the eastern region of the country, but a number of local municipalities and organizations nationwide now promote bird carving and art shows.

Waterfowl exhibits and competitions are not confined to the United States. Canada stages several very fine waterfowl shows each year

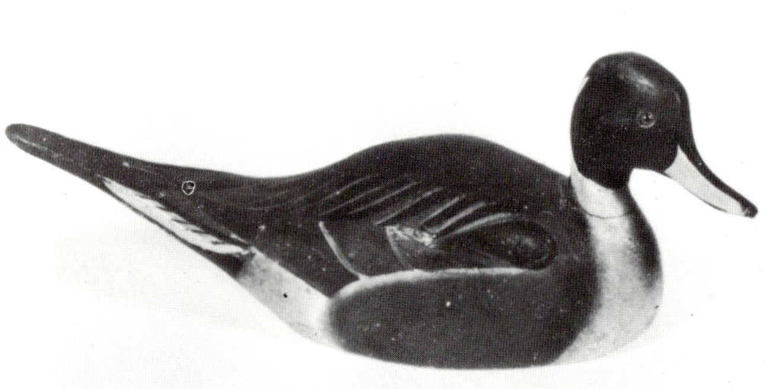

Pintail Drake - *Ward Brothers*

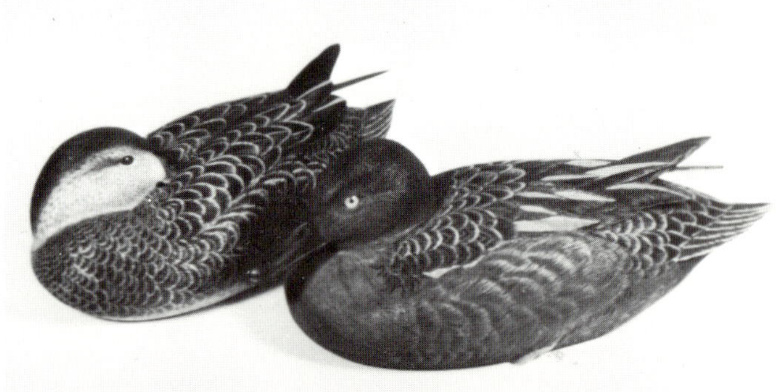

Mallards: Hen and Drake - *Tan Brunet*
Best in World Decorative Decoy Pair - *1978*

and many of their award winning and enthusiastic carvers also participate in the U.S. shows. Bird carving and collecting have also found new popularity in Great Britain.

Some of the finest bird carvers in the nation are from Michigan, where many of the top shows are hosted. Louisiana hosts some fine shows and in California, there are two shows each year. Pacific Southwest Wildfowl Arts promote a major show in San Diego in mid-February, and in late June, Sacramento hosts the Pacific Flyway Decoy Show. New York, Alabama, Ohio, New Jersey, North and South Carolina, Maryland and Virginia are some of the states where major wildfowl shows are held.

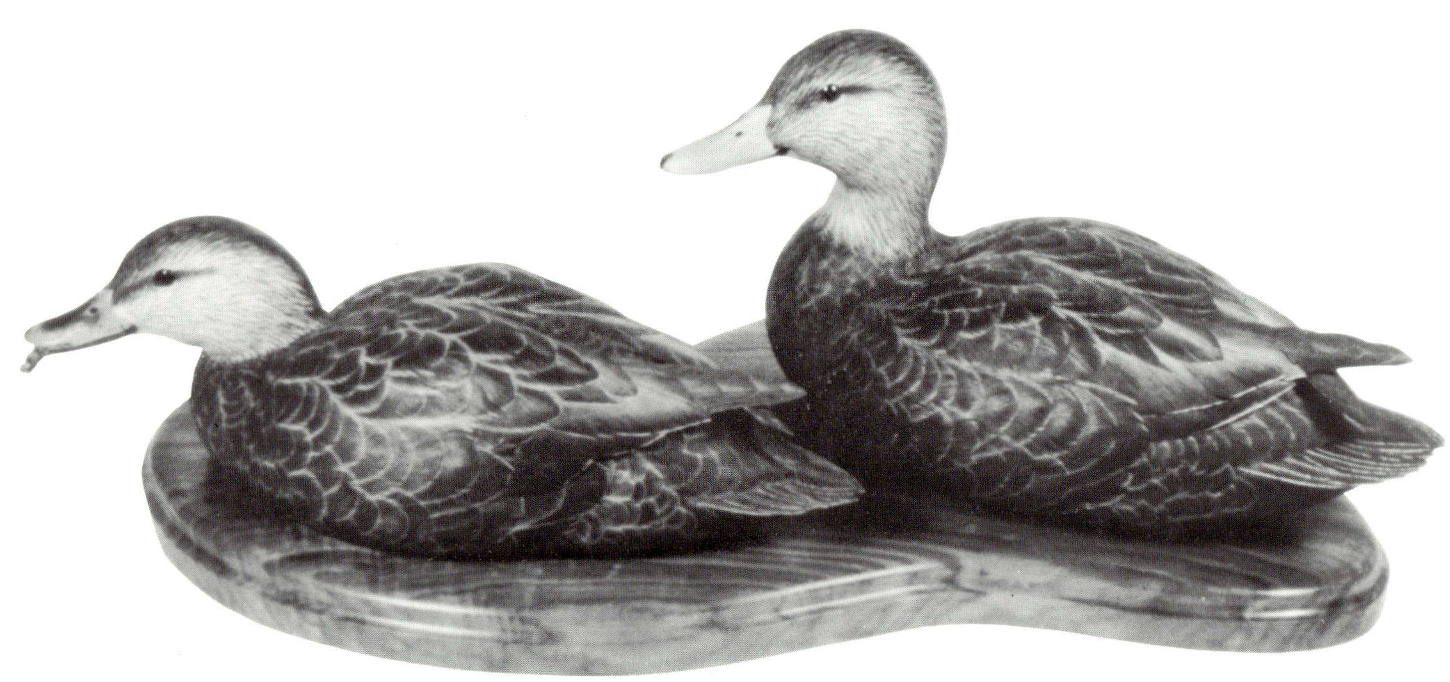

Black Ducks - *Pat Godin*, **Best in World Decorative Decoy Pair - *1980***

REFERENCE BOOKS

ALLEN, BONNIE - *Songbird Patterns*
ALLEN, BONNIE - *Songbird Patterns Book #2*
BARBER, GEORGE & READER, LARRY - *Decoy Carving Techniques for the Intermediate Carver*
BASILE, KENNETH & DOERZBACH, CYNTHIA - *American Decorative Bird Carving*
BERRY, ROBERT - *Decoy Patterns by Bob Berry*
BOWEN, FREDI - *Decorative Duck Painting (color charts)*
BRIDENHAGEN, KEITH & SPEILMAN, PATRICK - *Realistic Decoys, Carving, Texturing, Painting and Finishing*
BRIDENHAGEN, KEITH - *Decoy Pattern Book*
BURK, BRUCE - *Complete Water Studies, 3 volumes*
    Volume 1 - *Dabbling Ducks and Whistling Ducks*
    Volume 2 - *Diving Ducks*
    Volume 3 - *Geese and Swans*
    BURK, BRUCE - *Game Bird Carving, New Revised Edition*
BURK, BRUCE - *Waterfowl Studies*
BURK, BRUCE - *Decorative Decoy Designs*
CASSEDY, ED & CLODFELTER, KEN - *Carve-It, How to Carve a Green Wing Teal*
CASSON, PAUL W. - *Decoys Simplified*
CHAPPEL & SULLIVAN - *Wildlife Woodcarvers*
CONNETT, EUGENE - *Duck Decoys, How to Make Them, How to Paint Them, How to Rig Them*
DAISEY & KURMAN - *Songbird Carving*
FRANK, CHARLES W. - *Anatomy of a Waterfowl for Carvers and Painters*
GILLEY, WENDELL - *Art of Bird Carving*
GODIN, PATRICK - *Championship Waterfowl Patterns*
GREEN, H.D. - *Carving Realistic Birds*
GREEN, H.D. - *Patterns and Instructions for Carving Authentic Birds*
HILLMAN, ANTHONY - *Painting Duck Decoys*
HILLMAN, ANTHONY - *Carving Classic Regional Shorebirds*
HOLLATZ, TOM & DWYER, CORINE - *The Loon Book*
HOPPER, BEEBE - *Featherstrokes, The Basics of Painting Feathers*
HOPPER, BEEBE - *Featherstrokes for Canvasbacks*
HOPPER, BEEBE - *Featherstrokes for Mallards*
HOPPER, BEEBE - *Wildfowl Painting*
HAUSER, PRISCILLA - *Decorative Ducks*
HAUSER, PRISCILLA - *Decorative Ducks Volume #2*
KLEIN, TOM - *Loon Magic*
LADD, DAVE - *Creative Woodburning #11*
LADD, DAVE - *Wooden Ducks, An Artist's Portfolio*
LEHMAN, GEORGE - *20 Realistic Game & Songbird Wood Carving Patterns*
LEHMAN, GEORGE - *Realism in Wood*
LEHMAN, GEORGE - *Nature in Wood*
LEMASTER, RICHARD - *Decoys: The Art of the Wooden Bird*
LEMASTER, RICHARD - *Waterfowl - The Artists' Guide to Anatomy, Attitude and Color*
LEMASTER, RICHARD - *Wildlife in Wood*
LEMASTER, RICHARD - *Great Gallery of Ducks*
MOHRDART, DAVID - *Bird Reference Drawings*
MOHRDART, DAVID - *Bird Studies*
MURPHY, CHARLES F. - *Working Plans: Kit #1*
PHILLIPS, JOHN CHARLES - *A Nautral History of the Ducks*
PLAUMANN, FRED - *Selected Bird Patterns for Carvers*
PONTE, ALFRED H. - *Decoy Sculptures in Wood*
PONTE, ALFRED H. - *26 Realistic Duck Patterns*
SMALL, ANNE - *Masters of Bird Carving*
SCHROEDER, ROGER - *How to Carve Wildfowl*
SCHROEDER, ROGER - *How to Carve Wildfowl, Book 2*
SCHROEDER, ROGER - *Waterfowl Carving with J.D. Sprankle*
SCHROEDER, ROGER - *Songbird Carving with Ernest Muehlmatt*
SHOURDS, HARRY V. & HILLMAN, ANTHONY - *Carving Duck Decoys with Full Size Patterns for Hollow Construction*
SHOURDS, HARRY V. & HILLMAN, ANTHONY - *Carving Shorebirds*
SHOURDS, HARRY V. & HILLMAN, ANTHONY - *Exotic Decoys for the Woodcarver*
SPIELMAN, PATRICK - *Making Wood Decoys*
SPRANKLE, JIM - *Waterfowl Patterns and Painting*
STARR, DR. GEORGE R. - *How to Make Working Decoys*
SULLIVAN, CLARK & CHAPPEL - *Wildlife Wood Carvers Pattern Book, Drake & Puddle Ducks*
TODD, FRANK S. - *Waterfowl, Ducks, Geese and Swans of the World*
VEASEY, TRICIA - *Waterfowl Illustrated*
VEASEY, TRICIA - *Championship Carving*
VEASEY, TRICIA - *Championship Carving 1985 and 1986*
VEASEY, WILLIAM — *Waterfowl Carving, Blue Ribbon Techniques*
VEASEY, WILLIAM — *Waterfowl Painting, Blue Ribbon Techniques*
VEASEY, WILLIAM — *Blue Ribbon Burning Techniques*
VEASEY, WILLIAM & KURMAN, SINA - *Bills and Feet, An Artisan's Handbook*
WYLIE, STEPHEN & FURLONG, STEWARD - *Key to North American Waterfowl*

WILDFOWL EVENTS

The following is a partial listing of wildfowl shows that you might enjoy attending, including the location and month in which they are held.

January
Annapolis Wildfowl Carving and Art Exhibition
Annapolis, Maryland
Minnesota Decoy Collectors' Show
St. Paul, Minnesota
Suncoast Woodcarving Show
Pinellas Park, Florida

February
Pacific Southwest Wildfowl Arts California Open
San Diego, California
Long Island Decoy Collectors' Show
East Setauket, New York
Manasquan River Decoy Show
Wall Township, New Jersey
Minnesota Decoy Collectors' Show
Bloomington, Minnesota
Showcase of Woodcarving
Charlotte, North Carolina
Southeastern Wildlife Exposition
Charleston, South Carolina
Treasure Coast Woodcarving Club Exhibit
Port St. Lucie, Florida
Wildfowl Carving and Art Exhibition
Richmond, Virginia

March
Canadian National Decoy Carvers Competition
Toronto, Ontario, Canada
Delaware Wildlife Art Show
Newark, Delaware
Illinois Valley Wildlife Art Exhibition
Peoria, Illinois
Mahoning Valley Woodcarvers Exhibition
Warren, Ohio
Mid-Atlantic Wildfowl Festival
Virginia Beach, Virginia
Ohio Decoy Collectors and Carvers Show
Westlake, Ohio
Quebec Waterfowl Carving Contest
Montreal, Quebec, Canada
Rappahannock River Waterfowl Show
White Stone, Virginia

Texas Decoy and Wildfowl Festival
Dallas, Texas
Waterfowl and Wildlife Decoy Show
Tom's River, New Jersey
Wisconsin Decoy Collectors Show
Oshkosh, Wisconsin
Woodcarving and Wildlife Art Festival
Lancaster, Pennsylvania

April
World's Championship Wildfowl Carving Competition
Ocean City, Maryland
Chincoteague Island Easter Decoy Festival
Chincoteague, Virginia
Metro Carvers Woodcarving Show
Madison Heights, Michigan

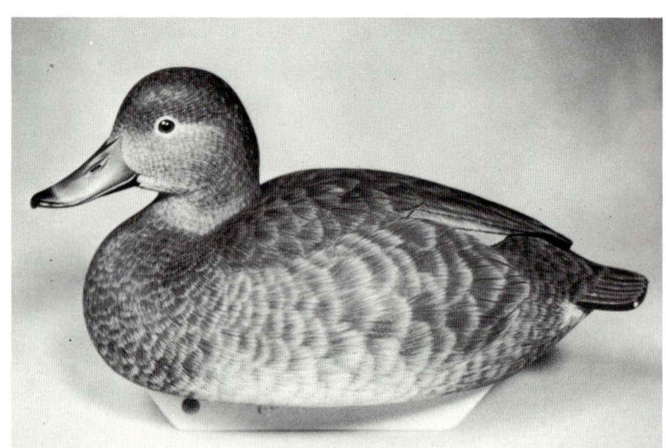

Cinnamon Teal: Hen - *James Sprankle* - **1979**

Michigan Wildlife Art Festival
Southfield, Michigan
Mid-Atlantic Woodcarving Show and Competition
Abington, Pennsylvania
Midwest Decoy Collectors Association
Chicago, Illinois
National Antique Decoy Collectors Show
Charles, Illinois
Wildlife '87
Upper Marlboro, Maryland
Wildlife and Western Art Exhibit
Minneapolis, Minnesota

May
Havre de Grace Decoy Festival
Havre de Grace, Maryland

Michigan Great Lakes Wildlife Festival
Clare, Michigan
Muleskinner Decoy Show
Clarence, New York
South Jersey Woodcarving Show
Millville, New Jersey

June
Onondaga Woodcarvers Club Show
Syracuse, New York
Pacific Flyway Decoy Association
Sacramento, California
Susquehanna Decoy Shop Outdoor
Woodcarving Show
Intercourse, Pennsylvania
Toronto Decoy Show
Toronto, Ontario, Canada

July
Cape May Waterfowl and Woodcarving Show
Cape May, New Jersey
Clayton Duck Decoy and Wildlife Art Show
Clayton, New York
New England Decoy Association
Hyannis, Massachusetts
Pacific Northwest Decoy Rally
Bellvue, Washington
Upper Midwest Woodcarvers Exhibition
Blue Earth, Minnesota

August
Buckhorn Wildlife Art Festival
Buckhorn, Ontario, Canada
Cajun Heritage Festival
Galliano, Louisiana
Canadian Agricultural International
Woodcarving Exhibition
Toronto, Ontario, Canada
Down East Carving and Art Festival
Rockport, Maine
International Decoy Contest
Davenport, Iowa
Michigan Hunting Decoy Contest
Davison, Michigan
Northwoods Decoy Collectors Show
Minocqua, Wisconsin
Southwestern Michigan Wildfowl Decoy
Competition
Delton, Michigan

West Coast Antique Decoy Collectors Show
and Sale
Monterey, California
The Wood Show
Durham, Ontario, Canada

September
Cape Cod Annual Bird Carvers Exhibit
Brewster, Massachusetts

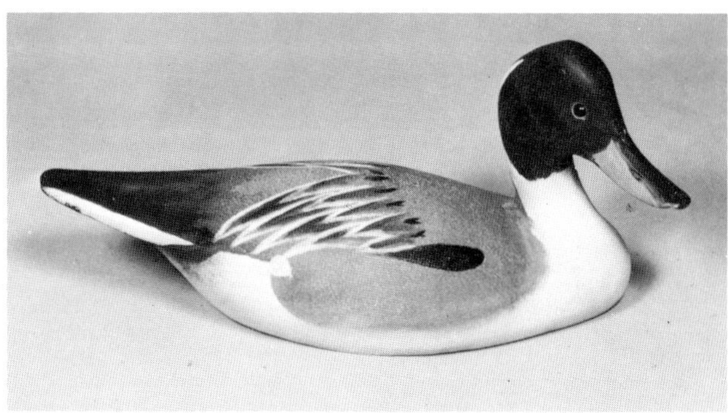

In the Collection - *Ward Foundation*

Currituck Wildlife Festival
Barco, North Carolina
Eddie Bauer Wildlife Art And Carvers Show
Seattle, Washington
Leigh Yawkey Woodson Art Museum "Birds
in Art" Exhibition
Wausau, Wisconsin
Louisiana Wildfowl Festival
New Orleans, Louisiana
Michigan Duck Hunters Tournament and
Decoy Contest
Pointe Mouille, Michigan
New Jersey Wings 'n Water Festival
Stone Harbor, New Jersey
North American Wildfowl Carving
Championships
Livonia, Michigan
Northern Lakes Decoy Show
Callaway, Minnesota
Ohio Duck Hunters and Decoy Tournament
Oak Harbor, Ohio
Old Time Barnegat Bay Decoy and Gunning
Show
Tuckerton, New Jersey
Pymatuning Waterfowl Exposition
Linesville, Pennsylvania
Wildlife and Sporting Art
Ligonier, Pennsylvania

WILDFOWL EVENTS

Yakima Regional Woodcarvers Rendezvous
Yakima, Washington
Yorkarvers Woodcarving and Decoy Show
York, Pennsylvania

October
Ward Foundation Wildfowl Carving and Art Exhibition
Salisbury, Maryland
Catahoula Lake Festival
Pineville, Louisiana
Chestertown Wildlife Show
Chestertown, Maryland
Garden State Wildfowl Carving and Exhibit
Little Silver, New Jersey
Kingfield-Gosfield South Migratory Festival
Kingville, Ontario, Canada
Little Sioux Shooting Blocks Decoy Contest
Cherokee, Iowa
North Carolina Waterfowl Weekend
Nags Head, North Calorina
Northwestern Michigan Wildlife Art Show
Traverse City, Michigan
Smokey Mountain Woodcarving Show
Pigeon Forge, Tennessee
Upper Shore Decoy Show
North East, Maryland

November
Artistry In Wood
Arlington, Virginia
Artistry In Wood
Glencoe, Illinois
Bird Carvers Exhibition and Sale
Worchester, Massachusetts
Long Island Wildfowl Carvers Exhibition
Amityville, New York
North Alabama Woodcarvers Show
Huntsville, Alabama
Northwest Carvers Association Woodcarving Show
Puyallup, Washington
Pennsylvania Wildlife Art Festival
York, Pennsylvania
Southern Wildfowl Festival
Decatur, Alabama

The Waterfow Festival
Easton, Maryland
Wild Birds In Wood
Portland, Oregon
December
Wildlife Art Exhibition and Sale
New Hope, Pennsylvania

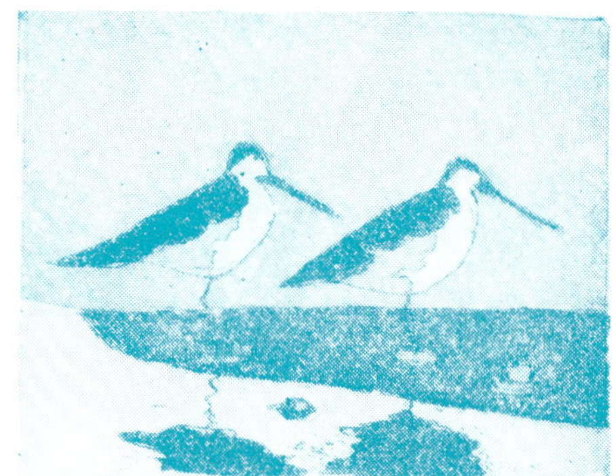

REFERENCE JOURNALS

PUBLICATIONS DEVOTED TO WILDLIFE CARVING AND ART

SCALE WOODCRAFT MAGAZINE
Dept. 1496
1000 Federal Road
Brookfield, CT 06804

WILDLIFE ART NEWS
P.O. Box 237
Elk River, MN 55330

WILDFOWL CARVING AND COLLECTING
P.O. Box 1831
Cameron and Kelker Sts.
Harrisburg, PA 17105

WILDFOWL ART JOURNAL OF THE WARD FOUNDAION
655 S. Salisbury Blvd.
Salisbury, MD 21801

BREAKTHROUGH
P.O. Box 1320
Loganville, GA 30249

DECOY HUNTER
901 N. 9th
Clinton, IN 47842

DECOY MAGAZINE
P.O. Box 1900
Montego Bay Station
Ocean City, MD 21842

PRINTS
P.O. Box 1468
Alton, IL 62002

BIBLIOGRAPHY

BIBLIOGRAPHY

Audubon Society Encyclopedia of North
American Birds

Fisher and Peterson - *The World of Birds*

Johnsgard - *A Guide of North American
Waterfowl*

Johnsgard - *Ducks, Geese and Swans of the
World*

Johnsgard - *Waterfowl of North America*

Kortright - *The Ducks, Geese & Swans of
North America*

Landsdowne - *Birds of the West Coast -
Volume 1*

Landsdowne - *Birds of the West Coast -
Volume 2*

Tunnicliff - *Tunnicliff Birds*

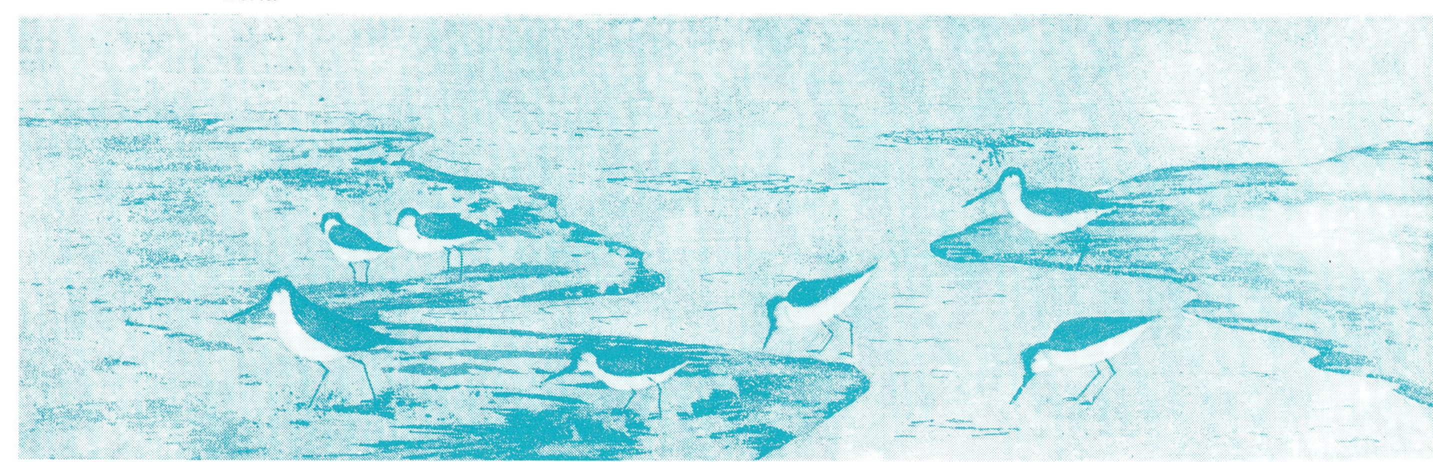

SOURCE LIST

SOURCES FOR MATERIALS

Al's Decoy Supplies
27 Connaught Avenue
London, Ontario, Canada
N5Y 3A4 (misc. supplies)

American Sales Co.
Box 741
Reseda, CA 91335
(misc. supplies)

Annex Mfg.
955 Blue Ball Rd.
Elkton, MD 21921
(wood burners)

Atlantic Flyway Decoy Co.
2248 Seashore Shops
Great Neck and Shore Drive
Virginia Beach, VA 23451
(misc. supplies)

Bred E. Bahr Lumber Co.
2460 S. Damen Ave.
Chicago, IL 60608
(wood)

Birdsall Decoys
723 Howe Street
Point Pleasant, NJ 08742
(machine blanks)

Birds of a Feather
Box 756
New Britain, CT 06050
(wooden bases)

Big Sky Carvers
8256 Huffine Lane
Bozeman, MT 59715
(machine blanks)

Bob Bolle
26421 Compson
Roseville, MI 48066
(cast study bills)

Books Plus
42 Charles St.
Lodi, NJ 07644
(books)

Canadian Woodworker, Ltd.
1391 St. James St.
Winnepeg, Manitoba, Canada
R3H 0Zl (misc. supplies)

Carvers Barn
P.O. Box 686 South Yarmouth
Cape Cod, MA 02664
(misc. supplies)

Carvers Corner
153 Passaic St.
Garfield, NJ 07026
(misc. supplies)

Carvers Eye
P.O. Box 16692
Portland, OR 97216
(glass eyes)

Chesterfield Craft Shop
P.O. Box 208, 20 Georgetown Rd.
Chesterfield, Trenton, NJ 08620
(misc. supplies, burners, feet)

Chez La Rogue
Rt. 3, Box 148
Foley, AL 36535
(misc. suppies)

Colwood Electronics
715 Westwood Ave.
Long Branch, NJ 17740
(wood burners)

Albert Constantine and Sons, Inc.
2050 Eastchester Rd.
Bronx, NY 10461
(misc. supplies)

Craft Cove, Inc.
2315 West Glen Avenue
Peoria, IL 61614
(misc. supplies)

Craftwoods
10921 York Rd.
Hunt Valley, MD 21030
(misc. supplies)

Curt's Waterfowl Corner
123 Le Boeuf St.
Montegut, LA 70377
(misc. supplies)

Richard Delise
920 Springwood Dr.
West Chester, PA 19380
(cast feet)

Dolington Woodcrafts
Washington Crossing
& Newtown Road
Newtown, PA 18940
(machine blanks)

Duck Blind
8721-B Gull Rd.
Richland, MI 49083
(waterfowl video tapes
& supplies)

The Duck Butt Boys
P.O. Box 2051
Metairie, LA 70004
(wood)

Duck Tape
Jim Reynolds
414 Emerson Rd.
Traverse City, MI 49684
(video tapes)

Electric Tool Service Co.
19442 Conant Ave.
Detroit, MI 48234
(misc. supplies)

Elkay Products Co., Inc.
1506 Sylvan Glade
Austin, TX 78745
(ruby cutters)

P.C. English Enterprises
P.O. Box 380
Thornburg, VA 22565
(misc. supplies)

Exotic Wood, Inc.
2483 Industrial St.
Burlingon, Ontario, Canada
L7P 1A6 (misc. supplies)

The Eyes
9630 Dundalk
Spring, TX 77379
(glass eyes)

Feather Merchants
279 Boston Post Rd.
Madison, CT 96443
(misc. supplies)

The Fine Tool Shops, Inc.
P.O. Box 1262
Danbury, CT 06810
(misc. supplies)

Foredom Electric Co.
Rt. 6
Bethel, CT 06801
(Foredom tool)

Forest Products
P.O. Box 12
Avon, OH 44011
(machine blanks)

Georgetown, Inc.
P.O. Box 625
Bethel Park, PA 15012
(videos tapes)

Gerry's Tool Shed
1111 Flint Rd., Unit 6
Downsview, Ontario, Canada
M3J 3C7 (misc. supplies)

Godin Art, Inc.
P.O. Box 62
Brantford, Ontario, Canada
N3T 5N3 (video tapes, books, supplies)

Greenwing Enterprises
Rt. 2, Box 731-B
Chester, MD 21619
(cast blanks, books)

John E. Heintz
6609 S. River Rd.
Marine City, MI 48039
(wildfowl photos)

Highwood Book Shop
P.O. Box 1246
Traverse City, MI 49685
(books)

Beebe and Jim Hopper
731 Beech Avenue
Chula Vista, CA 92010
(Permalba paints, Langnickel brushes, book

Christian J. Hummel Co.
404 Brooklets Ave.
Easton, MD 21601
(art supplies)

Hutch Decoy Carving, Ltd.
7715 Warsaw Ave.
Glen Burnie, MD 21061
(machine blanks)

The Jaymes Co.
10921 York Rd.
Hunt Valley, MD 21030
(knives)